D0184792

INCLUSION

IN THE

EARLY YEARS

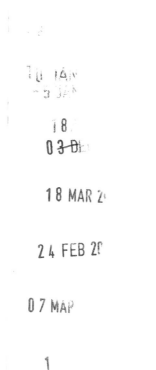

10 JAN
- 3 JAN

18
03 DE

18 MAR 2

24 FEB 20

07 MAR

1

372·216

Also available:

Behaviour in the Early Years: Tried and Tested Strategies
Angela Glenn, Jacquie Cousins and Alicia Helps
1-84312-336-3

Intervening Early: Promoting Positive Behaviour in Young Children
Nicky Hutchinson and Hilary Smith
1-84312-135-2

Working with Children in the Early Years
Jane Devereux and Linda Miller
1-85346-975-0

Supporting Children's Learning in the Early Years
Jane Devereux and Linda Miller
1-85346-976-9

Special Needs in Early Years Settings
Collette Drifte
1-85346-856-8

Removing Barriers to Learning in the Early Years: Tried and Tested Strategies
Angela Glenn, Jacquie Cousins and Alicia Helps
1-84312-338-X

Getting Ready to Read and Write in the Early Years: Tried and Tested Strategies
Angela Glenn, Jacquie Cousins and Alicia Helps
1-84312-337-1

INCLUSION
IN THE
EARLY YEARS:
stories of good practice

PHYLLIS JONES

 David Fulton Publishers

EAST DEVON COLLEGE
LIBRARY Cat
T23008 372.216

David Fulton Publishers Ltd
The Chiswick Centre, 414 Chiswick High Road, London W4 5TF

www.fultonpublishers.co.uk

First published in Great Britain in 2005 by David Fulton Publishers

David Fulton Publishers is a division of Granada Learning, part of ITV plc.

Note: The right of Phyllis Jones to be identified as the author of this work has been asserted by her in accordance with the Copyright, Designs and Patents Act 1988.

Copyright © Phyllis Jones 2005

British Library Cataloguing in Publication Data
A catalogue record for this book is available from the British Library.

ISBN 1-84312-121-2

10 9 8 7 6 5 4 3 2 1

All rights reserved. The material in this publication may be photocopied for use within the purchasing organisation. Otherwise, no part of this may be reproduced, stored in a retrieval system or transmitted, in any form or by any means, electronic, mechanical, photocopying, or otherwise, without the prior permission of the publishers.

Typeset by Kenneth Burnley, Wirral, Cheshire
Printed and bound in Great Britain by Ashford Colour Press

Contents

Acknowledgements

Clearly the major acknowledgements for this book have to go to the teachers, nursery nurses, teaching assistants and their pupils. They have shared their best lessons to help us to further our understanding and practice of teaching and learning with children who are different. They have willingly offered their planning and evaluations and engaged in frank reflections of their teaching. Without them, this book would never have been written. In addition, I would like to thank Bill for his proof reading and valuable editing comments. All of the names of children, adults and schools in this book have been changed to secure anonymity. Due to parental preference some children in the participating classes are not referred to in the text. Therefore, some of the classes described are in reality larger than the impression which may be given.

CHAPTER 1

Introduction: Setting the scene

The purposes of this book are many. First and foremost, it is intended as a sharing of examples of good practice in inclusive teaching and learning in the early years. It offers detailed practical scenarios of learning activities that have been planned and executed in order to include the full range of learning needs present in particular groups of children. When I was a deputy head teacher, I had responsibility for the organisation of the professional development opportunities for staff in the school where I worked. It was an exciting and salutary experience to find that staff learned most from each other. As trainers and managers, we can introduce theories, concepts and ideas about teaching and learning and about classroom management. But staff become much more engaged and animated when they listen to each other's journeys, reflect upon each other's practice and actually see a colleague translate theory into classroom practice. As a teacher myself, I enjoyed going into colleagues' classrooms and looking at the displays, the systems for planning and classroom management, and the children's work. What indeed I was experiencing was theory authenticated in practice. That is why this book, I believe, will appeal to practitioners. Here, we encounter examples of lessons that are authenticated in the real world. Moreover, these examples have been chosen as teachers' best lessons and, through this, offer a valuable insight into how effective inclusive teaching and learning is being perceived in some of our early years settings today.

The teachers we will meet in this book come from a range of early years settings that span rural, inner-city, segregated and mainstream contexts. You may wonder why segregated special schools are represented in a book about inclusive teaching. Surely, I can hear some of you saying, inclusion should be about mainstreaming children? Indeed, the involvement of special schools has been deliberate. It is a personal attempt 'not to throw the baby out with the bath water' in respect of effective teaching and learning strategies. It is intended to show and reinforce the idea that excellent inclusive teaching and learning happens across many different contexts of provision. We have a great deal to learn from each other about effective teaching and learning. We must be willing to enter into dialogue with each other to extend and to develop our understanding and practice of inclusion.

As we learn more about inclusion and inclusive practice, we learn more about its complexity, its challenges and its difficulties. Inclusion is not easy: its challenges confront many of us daily. It can be a relief (and a delight) to share in the good practice of others in this most challenging process. What we do know is that collaboration is a very supportive framework in which to develop our own understanding and skills. It is in this spirit of collaboration that the special schools (along with their good practice) earned their place in this book. Ultimately, in an ideal inclusive world, all our children would be given a challenging and appropriate education in their local community school. The reality of current provision is that we need to learn more about how we can include a diverse range of learners in appropriate and exciting teaching and learning, whatever the context. One of the ways to do this is to listen to, and learn from, the people who are engaging in authentic inclusive teaching and learning now.

The book is structured to enable a similar format to be followed in each teacher's account of her best inclusive lesson (all of the teachers, through coincidence rather than design, are female). This is done to support cohesion and to promote potential similarities and differences emerging across the range of learning contexts. However, you will see that each teacher emphasises different things. This is a representation of the different styles and strengths of individual teachers, as well as a reflection of the larger differing school contexts in which they work. Chapters 2 and 3 offer an insight into the policy and theoretical issues that impact upon the contexts in which the teachers work. In Chapter 2, the key principles of the *SEN Code of Practice* (DfES, 2001a) and the *Disability Discrimination Act* (DHSS, 2001) are discussed in relation to the development of greater inclusive practice. These include individual needs, mainstream or inclusive placement, the views of children, the views of parents and the entitlement to a broad and balanced curriculum. Chapter 3 discusses some of the main ideas and concepts that relate to inclusive practice in the early years. It sets out what we mean when we say a child has a special educational need. There follows a discussion of differentiation as an essential component in creating greater inclusive practice. The chapter ends by looking at models of early years organisation and how these may best support further inclusive practice. Chapters 4 through to 7 present the accounts of the teachers' best lessons. In Chapter 8 the similarities and differences between the accounts of the best lessons are discussed. In doing so, key issues will be highlighted in relation to the nature of inclusive teaching and learning, and the possible lessons we can learn about meeting the teaching and learning needs of diverse groups of early years learners. A glossary of terms used in the book is included, in order to support the shared understanding of terminology.

Teachers were given information at the beginning of their involvement in the book, in order to help them decide upon, prioritise and sort the information they offered for the book. Although the information given to the teachers was simple and clear, they were given the freedom to interpret how they wanted to contribute. No set format for planning was given to the teachers to allow them to present the planning processes that they operated in their different contexts. The different narratives represent how the different teachers are understanding and perceiving inclusive practice. The teachers were free to choose their own 'best' lesson, so the accounts that follow are indeed personal to each of the teachers and reflect their own interpretations of 'best' practice. It is necessary at this point to consider the following:

- persuasion of the teachers to be part of the book (and indeed the children and other staff in the settings);
- contextual information about the schools and classes where the best lessons take place. This includes the information teachers were asked to provide about the schools, classes, children and adults;
- planning information, documents, etc. that the teachers were asked to provide, and why;
- account of the teaching and learning, including the range of additional material teachers could include to illustrate and exemplify their best lesson accounts; and
- evaluation and reflection by teachers offering an insight into why they felt this was their 'best' inclusive lesson.

Persuasion of the teachers to be part of the book

All of the teachers in the book work in the north east of England. The teachers involved had a reputation at my university as effective early years teachers, who were including a range of different learners in their teaching. The focus of the book demanded that such a reputation was important to reflect best practice. Understandings and perceptions about what is best practice may differ, but what the teachers in this book share is a willingness to include children who learn differently. There is a keenness to want to be responsive to the individual needs of children and to help all the children in their class to be successful as learners. The teachers in this book share all of these traits and have a reputation for being successful in their endeavours.

As soon as individual teachers were approached it became obvious that, due to the nature of early years provision, we were not talking about one individual early educator, but a team of adults who worked collaboratively in the classes. Initially, the project was presented to the head teacher or manager of the provision, and once permission had been gained, individual team leaders (who were indeed the teachers of the class) were approached. The busy context of an early years class does not make one keen to take on extra work, so it was important to demonstrate to each teacher the potential value of the book and offer clear guidance concerning the level of their contribution. Following a discussion, a brief information sheet about the project and the extent of their participation was prepared and left with the teacher. She then went to the team to ask for their thoughts and to ascertain their willingness to participate in the project. The teams of adults in the classes varied, and this will be further described in the forthcoming chapters.

Once initial interest was shown, appropriate permission was sought from the parents and children of the settings. Some schools already had whole class permission to be involved in a range of university or action research projects. Some parents chose not to have their children included. These children participated in the lessons as usual, but we did not include them in the retelling of the account. Everyone was assured that names would be changed to protect anonymity and confidentiality.

Contextual Information

In the very early planning stages of the book, it was considered important to try to represent the range of early years classes we may encounter in practice. Therefore, it became important to aim to represent a diverse range of provision for children in the early years. This was achieved by careful consideration of the context of the school. It was decided to use a mixture of segregated, mainstream, rural and inner-city settings to present a manageable but substantially varied range of provision. Clearly, this does not represent all of the different types of early years contexts, but it does offer a mixture varied enough for us to appreciate the nature of differences in practice. The best lesson accounts we will hear about range from early years day nurseries (funded through Early Years Childcare Partnerships) through to Reception classes. The range of early years classes in the book is illustrated in Table 1.1.

Classroom 1 is known as Summerfield Glade School. It is a nursery or Reception class within a segregated rural special school. The school caters for pupils aged four to nineteen years with severe and profound and multiple learning difficulties. Owing to small numbers of children overall in the school, it is not uncommon in the segregated sector to

Table 1.1 The range of early years classes

	Rural	Inner city	Nursery	Reception
Segregated	Classroom 1: Summerfield Glade School	Classroom 3: Blackberry Hill School	Classroom 1: Summerfield Glade School	Classroom 1: Summerfield Glade School
			Classroom 3: Blackberry Hill School	Classroom 3: Blackberry Hill School
Mainstream	Classroom 2: Springfield First School	Classroom 4: Riverview Primary School	Classroom 2: Springfield First School	Classroom 4: Riverview Primary School

find children of wide age differences (four to six years) in the same class. This particular class has a wide age range, spanning from early nursery to late Reception.

Classroom 2 is known as Springfield First School. It is a part-time nursery within a small rural primary school.

Classroom 3 is known as Blackberry Hill School. It is a nursery reception class within an inner-city segregated special school. The school caters for pupils aged four to eleven years with learning difficulties. Again, the spread of ages in one class is greater than in a mainstream setting. The school is situated on the outskirts of a large city and takes children from across the borough.

Classroom 4 is known as Riverview Primary School. It is a Reception class in a large inner-city primary school. The school is situated towards the centre of a large city and takes children from a small catchment area which has a low socio-economic profile. A high percentage of all the children attending the school are on free school meals. The Reception class is a county-funded, additionally resourced provision to support children with speech and language difficulties.

In addition to the profiles of the range of classes offered in Table 1.1, each teacher's account of her best lesson includes more details about settings in which she teaches. This includes the larger professional context in which the chosen classes operate. Therefore, general information about the school was included; this information comes from school booklets, profiles, Ofsted reports, etc. The focus of the contextual information then moves to the class itself. The classroom or nursery context is described. Information about staff qualifications and experience is presented to show the nature of the adult experience in the class. Contextual information about the children themselves is then described. In some cases, this is on an individual basis, and in others it is general information about the class of children and then more specific information about individual children. This may include the stage of the *Code of Practice* the child is on, and brief information about their strengths and different learning needs

Planning

To reflect on the accounts of the 'best lessons', it is important for the lessons themselves to be set out in relation to long-, medium- and short-term planning processes adopted. The longer- and medium-term planning offers a curriculum context for the more immediate shorter-term planning. The shorter-term planning demonstrates how curriculum demands and individual needs are going to be engaged with in the lesson through the stated aims and objectives of the lesson. The planning material ranges across appropriate elements in the Foundation Curriculum, Early Learning Goals, school and class schemes of work, activity plans and Individual Education Plans (IEPs).

Accounts of the 'best' lesson

All teachers were asked to give a simple and clear descriptive account of the lesson, an account that anyone could read and obtain a feel for what actually happened in the lesson. Such a description needed to paint a picture of the best lesson from beginning to end. Teachers were encouraged to exemplify this with photographs of the children in the lesson or examples of children's work.

Evaluation of the lesson

All teachers were asked to provide an evaluation of the lesson. They were encouraged to evaluate the lesson in relation to the stated aims and objectives and also include information about why this lesson was chosen to demonstrate their best inclusive lesson. Insights into possible reasons why the lesson was seen as their best are particularly important to this book. First, it allows us to appreciate why practice is seen as good by experienced teachers; and second, it allows us to look for possible themes that may run through all the chapters in the book – themes that may help us develop greater awareness of the nuances and subtleties of effective inclusive practice.

CHAPTER 2

Principles of the
Code of Practice

INTRODUCTION

The key principles of the *SEN Code of Practice* (DfES, 2001a) and *Disability Discrimination Act* (DHSS, 2001) will be discussed in relation to the development of greater inclusive practice. These include individual needs, mainstream or inclusive placement, the views of children, the views of parents and the entitlement to a broad and balanced curriculum.

The *SEN Code of Practice* (DfES, 2001a)

One of the most recent pieces of legislation sets out the statutory duties required from local education authorities (LEAs), health authorities, etc., to identify, assess and provide for a child's special educational needs. It also sets out the arrangements for the assessment, planning and recording procedures a school or early years provider should adopt. This is the framework by which children are assessed and issued with Statements of Special Educational Need. Statements of Special Educational Need are legal documents that set out individual needs and the provision required by the LEA to meet those needs. It is indeed the only legal document that parents can use as a form of recourse against an LEA. The *Code* was revised from an old model and its release was delayed in order for it to integrate the Disability Discrimination Act (DHSS, 2001). The *Code* offers guidance on the different phases of education: early years, primary, and secondary. The *Code* promotes a graduated response to the provision for special educational needs through the different phases of Early Years Action, Early Years Action Plus, School Action and School Action Plus. The Act offers a stronger right for children with special educational needs to be educated in a mainstream school, while it assigns duties to LEAs, schools and nursery settings to involve parents actively in the decision-making process. It also presents a new right for schools to request a statutory assessment of a child. There are some key fundamental principles of the *SEN Code of Practice* that relate to individual needs, mainstream placement or inclusion, child and parent perspectives and the entitlement to a broad and balanced curriculum.

Principle 1: Individual needs

The first principle of the *Code* refers to the statement that children with special educational needs must have their needs met. This may seem rather obvious, but the very fact that it is in the Act tells a salutary story of children who have indeed not had their special educational needs met. Growing numbers of successful litigation cases brought against LEAs by parents who feel strongly that their child's needs have not been met support this. You may have talked with parents, fellow professionals and practitioners about children who have been included in a mainstream setting that did not meet their individual strengths; indeed, sometimes these children are referred to as the victims of inclusion. It is these children who make the first principle of the *Code of Practice* so crucial to the provision of effective inclusive practice.

Differentiation refers to the way teaching and learning is planned and executed in order to meet individual learning needs. Therefore, in the development of greater inclusive practice, differentiation is an essential component. In an integration model, differentiation is concerned with how individual needs are married to curriculum demands, where the onus is on the child to change, to conform to the curriculum standards and expectations. In an inclusion model, differentiation is much more flexible. It is about how the curriculum needs are married to individual learning strengths and needs, where diversity is celebrated and honoured. Corbett (2001) discusses the process of differentiation as connective pedagogy that should be an inherent part of all planning: a pedagogy that involves teacher beliefs, attitudes, knowledge, skills and understanding in a bridge between the demands of the curriculum and the individual needs of the child. When we talk about pedagogy, we talk about something greater than teaching. Alexander (2000) suggests that it is important to clarify the difference between teaching and pedagogy and suggests that pedagogy involves the performance of teaching as well as the theories, beliefs, policies and controversies that inform such teaching. Therefore, when we plan for different learners we need to be aware of the impact of our attitudes and beliefs in order to engage in the connective pedagogy highlighted by Corbett (2001). Differentiation is multi-faceted:

*   it can occur for an individual or for a group of children;
*   it can be fluid (groups changing on a regular basis);
*   it can be static (groups remaining the same for a period of time);
*   it can be planned in meticulous detail before the teaching and learning occur (referred to as planned differentiation); and
*   it can be based on a child's response and engagement to a task (referred to as differentiation by outcome).

Most important to remember is that differentiation should be about the child and teacher working collaboratively in an informed way to develop optimal learning strategies. Some of the strategies and processes involved in differentiation can be best illustrated through questions:

- How is the task developmentally appropriate for the child?
- How does the task challenge the child?
- How does the task represent strengths in learning as well as difficulties?
- How does the task represent differences in the learning styles of the child?
- How are the resources deployed to support optimal child engagement?
- How is the learning organised to support optimal child engagement?
- How is the learning organised to support co-operative and collaborative learning?
- How are the assessment strategies managed to celebrate progress and achievement?
- How transparent and clear is the process of differentiation?
- How are the perspectives of the child (and families) integrated into the differentiation?
- How do the evaluation strategies help the teacher to reflect on the processes of learning as well as the products of learning?

Principle 2: Mainstream or inclusive placement

A second principle of the legislation specifically relates to placement. It states that the special educational needs of disabled children will normally be met in mainstream schools or settings. Now, this is a subtle but significant change in legislation. Before this, a child with a Statement of Special Education would normally be placed in special education provision, and then would need to have a case made to be educated in a mainstream setting. However, through this Act, this scenario has been turned on its head. Now a child would need to have a case made to be educated in a segregated context.

It was Mary Warnock in the late 1970s who introduced the term 'continuum of special educational need' that spanned across all school provision (DES, 1978). In this continuum she discussed 20 per cent of children requiring some form of special educational provision at some point in their school career, with 2 per cent of these children being placed in segregated schooling. This was a very powerful report that opened up the concept of special educational need being applied to children who spend their whole educational career in mainstream schools. For many years this report dominated educational debate. A major aspect of the report was the classification of children into different categories of learning difficulty: mild, moderate and severe, with educational provision generally matching these categories. So a child with mild learning difficulties would usually have been in mainstream, a child with moderate learning difficulty (MLD) would usually have been placed in a special school for MLD, and a child with severe learning difficulties (SLD) would usually have attended a special school for SLD. We can see from this that, historically, the categorization of a special educational need has had a great impact on the nature of the educational provision available to a child. This makes the recent increase in the emphasis on categories by the Department for Education and Science a retrograde and worrying step (see Chapter 3).

Warnock (DES, 1978) also offered a model of integration that continues to be helpful to us in our current understanding and quest to develop greater inclusive practices. She offered a three-tiered model of integration:

- *Tier 1: local.* This is where the child is geographically located with children of the same age in a local primary school. It may be a separate unit, building or class, but the intention was that local interaction would occur. However, in practice such units operated very differently and rarely would children meet to interact.
- *Tier 2: social.* This is where opportunities for social exchange between children in a segregated setting and children in a mainstream setting would be orchestrated. In the 1970s and 1980s there were parties galore in the name of social integration. Lots of fun to be had by all, but with no real sustained interaction between the children.
- *Tier 3: functional.* This is where a child with special educational needs attends a mainstream school for limited, but supported, time. The child would need to manage the work, with adaptations. Unfortunately, because of the location of segregated provision, this integration tended to be in schools that were local to the special school rather than their home community.

In the twenty or so years since the report, there has been a significant shift in the understanding of disability rights issues which is interrelated with understandings of equal opportunities issues (Hughes, 1998). These new and different understandings have challenged the notion of integration as advocated by Warnock. A major influencing factor in this change has been the impact of work emerging from the disability movement, particularly in respect to human rights and political perspectives (Oliver, 1996; Barnes, 1996). These have disputed theories that focus on individual problems and ownership of disability, and have initiated a debate where disabled people are the major stakeholders. This has been discussed within the paradigm of the social theory of disability. Medical and social theories of disability have emerged as different and opposing models of understanding that are seen to drive practice.

The word 'inclusion' (DfEE, 1998a) began to appear in literature and government documentation. Notions of inclusion relate to the social model of disability where the onus is on accepting and valuing all people in society and understanding the impact of the community on disability. The potential implications of accepting the notion of inclusion rather than integration are significant for an organisation because inclusion appears to demand a process of change for the whole community; this in itself transcends the notion of integration (Reiser and Mason, 1992). Central to inclusion is the demand to challenge constantly the *status quo*, personal assumptions and perceptions (Swain *et al.*, 1998). Inherent in the process of inclusion is a prerequisite of the need to listen to people who are directly involved and experience the services. From this, it appears that the concept of inclusion relates to a social model of disability that transcends individual services and becomes pertinent to the development of society in a global context (Mittler, 2000). There is documented evidence to suggest that there is confusion between the terms 'integration' and 'inclusion' (Thomas and Loxley, 2001). It is important that, as developers of greater inclusive practice, we are aware of this confusion and in our practice be aware of the differences.

Recently, another term, 'social inclusion' (Acheson, 1998) has also been adopted. This is explicitly linked to social exclusion, which relates to wider societal issues of health, poverty, vulnerability and disadvantage (Mittler, 2000). The Cabinet Social Exclusion Unit illustrates the government commitment to the reduction of social exclusion (Mittler, 2000) and this is also evident in major intervention initiatives from the government (Sure Start, Early Excellence Centres, Parenting Education and Support Programmes). Issues related to educational inclusion and social inclusion are seen to be interlinked and offer a philosophical basis for pursuing educational inclusion – to influence the wider social inclusion debate and practice. In this debate the whole question of whether inclusive schools are effective schools comes into play. This is an essential component of the future of greater inclusive practice. If we can show that inclusive schools benefit all and are effective for all learners, then the journey towards developing more inclusive schools will be helped enormously.

Principle 3: The views of children

A third principle of the legislation refers to the importance of listening to the perspective of children. It states that the views of the child should be sought and taken into account and establishes the principle of actively seeking the views of children themselves. There is a great deal we can learn by listening to children. At a conference on inclusive education one young person with learning difficulty articulated the following wise words: 'We believe that the best people to talk about having a learning difficulty and our rights are those with learning difficulties' (Souza, 1994 in Murray and Penman, 1996, p. 55).

The People First Organisation is an example of the developing practice in this area of actively listening to young people with disabilities and serves to illustrate the great contribution people with learning disabilities can make when circumstances allow it. There have been some significant developments in our understanding of enabling pupils with severe learning disabilities to participate in decision-making (Rose *et al.*, 1999). There is also a small body of research in the area of listening to learning disabled children (Cook and Swain, 2001; Wade and Moore, 1993). One young man with cerebral palsy wrote of his experiences that underlined his frustration with the attitudes of other people: 'I have cerebral palsy. I am fourteen years old. My parents treat me like a normal person. My biggest problem is other people's attitudes towards me' (Somogyvary, 1986, p. 30 in Wade and Moore, 1993).

As practitioners, we need to find creative ways to enable younger children with special educational needs to express their views about our work with them. In addition, we need to be prepared to hear things that may potentially challenge our current practice and understanding.

Principle 4: The views of parents

A fourth principle of the legislation refers to the role of parents. We know parents have a vital role to play in supporting their child's education. Involving parents in their child's education is not a new concept by any means. The role of partnerships with families has always been a significant element of services in the early years, particularly in family centres (Bruce *et al.*, 2001). This is borne out in the more recent consultation paper entitled *Every Child Matters* that is a framework which sets out to improve 'Outcomes for all children and their families, to protect them, to promote their well-being and to support all children to develop their full potential' (DfES, 2003, p. 53).

However, in reality, it is something with which professionals continue to struggle (Jones and Swain, 1999; Clarke and Jones, 2000). Current issues and dilemmas appear less to be about the principle of including parents, but more to do with the quality, depth and efficacy of this involvement. A brief look at the literature in the area of parental perspectives about the concept of parent involvement offers a valuable insight into how some parents actually think professionals are doing. Fitton (1994) offers two eloquent, but very different, perspectives of her daughter who had the classification of profound and multiple learning difficulties: one for professionals and one for friends. The professional perspective stressed the negative problems that her daughter so clearly had: the fits, the physical deformities, the feeding problems; a deficit-driven definition of her daughter. The second perspective intended for friends stressed her daughter's positive attributes: her sense of humour, her successful communication strategies, her mischief, her preferences, etc.; a positive attribute-driven definition of her daughter. On reading both descriptions it would be easy to assume that they were two different children! This tension between professional and parental views of disabled children is further supported in this poem by a mother of a young boy with profound and multiple disabilities:

When you look at my child

What do you see
When you look at my child?
How does he make you feel?

Your words confirm what I see in your eyes
Confident words, so secure
In the assumptions that you make.

Which child are you speaking about?

What do you see
When you look at me?
How do I make you feel?

Your manner suggests the response you expect
So sure of your words, Taking
For granted the role that you choose.

Are you really talking to me?

When did I tell you I wanted him changed
That I would prefer him different
From as he is?
When did I tell you I wanted your help
To change him?
I longed for my child for such a long time
I met him and chose him
And held my breath for a while.
I was very lucky.
He decided I belonged to him too.

Why would I change him?

> Don't you realise that I can feel
> Your need to change him
> Your need for him to be other than what he is
> To be 'improved'
> To be more or less or whatever
> You are disturbed by?
>
> Don't you understand that
> The comments you make about my child
> Tell about yourself
> And not about him?
>
> And the needs we discuss
> Are yours
> And not his.
>
> When you look at my child.
>
> (Murray and Penman, 1996, p. 4)

In this poem there is clear anger from the mother at professionals for making assumptions about her son. This mother is talking proudly about her son. His disabilities are an intrinsic part of his being and she does not take kindly to professionals wanting to change him. The work of Carpenter (1998) offers another valuable insight into the feelings and emotions of parents of children with disabilities and raises particular issues related to grief and vulnerability. What can we as professionals learn from these examples of tension? We can accept that parental perspectives can be different from our own and that they may even clearly challenge our current understandings and practice, but what status do we actually give to these perspectives?

Principle 5: Entitlement to a broad and balanced curriculum

A fifth principle of the *Code* states that children with special educational needs should be offered full access to a broad, balanced and relevant education, including an appropriate curriculum for the Foundation Stage and the National Curriculum. Again, this is not a new concept. Thirty years ago children with severe learning difficulty (a proportion of children with special educational needs) were the sole responsibility of Health (Lacey, 1991). It can be assumed from this that the children were judged to be trainable but ineducable. It was the 1970 Education Act that moved the responsibility of their education to the Department for Education. Junior training centres changed their names overnight to special schools. However, the practice in the special schools was seen to remain the same with an emphasis on skills training. Lacey (1991) offers an historical analysis of the way the curriculum has been designed for children with special educational needs and presents a clear picture of what was happening in special schools in the 1970s and 1980s. Their work illustrates the emphasis on highly focused and direct teaching of each and every new skill. Teachers devised and followed extremely detailed individual learning programmes with an adherence to developmental psychology based on normal development. This is also evident in approaches for working with very young children with special educational needs. Portage is a fine example of this (and is still employed today), where a developmentally based curriculum forms the central focus of a collaborative planning and teaching process based in the home setting.

The Warnock Report (1978) formed the bedrock of the 1981 Education Act where there was an emphasis on matching educational need with educational provision. This was (and still is) described in a Statement of Special Educational Need. A Statement of Special Educational Need is a legally binding contract between parents and LEAs. It sets out the learning needs of the child, as presented through a multi-professional assessment, and the appropriate provision deemed appropriate to meet those needs. The behavioural processes of assessment, teaching and evaluation advocated in the Act can be seen to reflect the teaching practices in the special schools (Ouvrey and Saunders, 1996) and therefore tended to confirm current practices.

The Education Reform Act (1988) heralded the National Curriculum, a curriculum to which every child was entitled, even children attending special schools. This formed the precursor for a process of curriculum change in special schools where teachers attempted to marry the National Curriculum to the individual needs of their pupils (Carpenter *et al.*, 1996). In practice, this Act had an important influence on the understanding of teachers of pupils with special educational needs, as it served as a critique of the special school curriculum they had delivered for so many years. In attempting to marry the demands of the National Curriculum to the individual learning needs of children, issues related to breadth and balance were addressed (Carpenter *et al.*, 1996). What the National Curriculum lacked was developmental detail, which benefited special schools, since there was a lack of prescription. However, the introduction of the Standard Assessment Tasks (SATs) relating to the National Curriculum and the beginning of the accountability debate in schools appeared to work against special schools. It became clear very quickly that there was an emerging tension between the SATs and children with special educational needs: 'SATs are being piloted in selected special schools, but it appears that they are generally considered to be unsuitable, in their present form, for many pupils with special educational needs' (Lacey, 1991, p. 67).

Several changes occurred to highlight and support the needs of children with identified special education at this time. The 1994 *Code of Practice* is an example of educational policy focusing directly upon the needs of disabled children. With its emphasis on supporting children in the mainstream, it fuelled the whole differentiated learning debate. The 1996 Education Act offered a 'slimmed down' version of the National Curriculum that was intended to offer flexibility and creativity. This, along with the Dearing Report (1994), that was to allow teaching from different key stages, where appropriate, helped to alleviate the rising tension around SATs for children with special educational needs. This was quite significant: it allowed teachers to teach from earlier key stages, which they felt were more appropriate to the developmental and intellectual needs of their pupils. This, to some extent, enabled the National Curriculum to be applied more creatively and flexibly.

However, the advent of Ofsted, the National Literacy Strategy (NLS) and National Numeracy Strategy (NNS) with their driving aim to improve standards in numeracy and literacy, can be seen to offer a real challenge to teachers and demanded that they develop more creative and flexible practices for children with special educational needs. They have proved to be substantial policy documents for all pupils with disabilities. It was an accepted principle that all children would participate in these strategies, and teachers of all pupils needed to be able to manage the strategies effectively (Berger *et al.*, 2000). Ofsted, as the government inspection machine, would inspect them. Any school not effectively developing these strategies as intrinsic parts of the National Curriculum would be adversely reported upon. Carpenter states that, in the 2001 national Ofsted report for special schools, it was acknowledged 'that many schools still need to make further improvements to ensure that all pupils have access to the full National Curriculum' (Carpenter *et al.*, 2001, p. 9).

The late 1990s and beyond have brought a 'quasi commercial' world of education (Aird, 2001) where the agenda is set squarely on raising standards, with an emphasis upon showing progress and measuring value for money through notions of value added. For children with special educational needs, this is an opportunity to measure their progress in small steps. Unfortunately, the machinery of all schools is designed to illustrate this with the prominence on testing and publication of results. However, the QCA project (2001) illustrates a milestone in policy development; it was developed out of a collaborative research process that has, as its central focus, the views of teachers of children with severe and profound and multiple learning disabilities. It sets out advice and guidelines whereby teachers will be able to demonstrate progress through teacher assessment of level descriptors (P levels). The guidelines can be seen as a process that will enable teachers of children with special educational needs to participate more fully in the raising of standards and school improvement agenda. They also offer a wealth of information that can be employed by the teacher to develop greater differentiated learning. It breaks down the skills and stages of the National Curriculum into more achievable goals for children experiencing difficulty in learning. Guidelines relating to very young children are still awaited, but what is currently available can still be used creatively by teachers and professionals.

CONCLUSION

The key principles of the *SEN Code of Practice* (DfES, 2001a) and *Disability Discrimination Act* (DHSS, 2001) have been discussed in detail, with particular reference to the development of greater inclusive practice. These included individual needs, mainstream or inclusive placement, the views of children, the views of parents and the entitlement to a broad and balanced curriculum. These key principles can be seen to be helpful in developing greater understanding of inclusive practice, as they can be seen to ask us not only to consider our practice, but also our belief systems and the policy frameworks which influence them.

Key issues in the literature and research

INTRODUCTION

This chapter discusses some of the main ideas and concepts that relate to inclusive practice in the early years. It will begin by setting out what we mean when we say a child has a special educational need. There follows a discussion of differentiation as an essential component of creating greater inclusive practice. The chapter ends by looking at models of early years organisation and how these may best support further inclusive practice.

Learning difficulty and special educational need

There is a variety of common terms that are in regular use in schools and services today used to group, label and categorise young children. These are: 'learning difficulty'; 'special educational need'; 'disability' (as in a child with a physical disability); and 'impairment' (as in a child with a visual impairment). Naturally, these are overarching to numerous individual syndromes that we may come across in school. It is not helpful to try to know all the syndromes, many of them being rare and medically based. However, it is important to be aware of some of the main ones and to know where to go for information about those we encounter with which we are unfamiliar. Contact a Family (www.cafamily.org.uk) is a wonderful source of information here. This is an organization set up to support parents, families, professionals and practitioners. It lists the thousands of current syndromes, along with brief information about the syndrome and valuable contact information to support parents' groups in the country. The desire to label and classify has worryingly even resulted in the creation of a syndrome 'SWAN': Syndrome Without A Name! This syndrome offers no specific educational or social information about the nature of the child's strengths or needs, but allows the child to be classified and labelled.

'Learning difficulty' and 'special educational needs' are two terms that are used together. Currently, a child is deemed to have a special educational need, referred to as a learning difficulty, if they:

- have a significantly greater difficulty in learning than the majority of children the same age; or
- have a disability that prevents or hinders them from making use of educational facilities of a kind generally provided for children of the same age, in schools within the area of the LEA;
- are under compulsory school age and fall within either of the above, or will do so if special educational provision is not made for them.

Special educational provision means:

- For children age two or over, educational provision which is additional to, or otherwise different from, the educational provision made generally for children of their age in schools maintained by the LEA, other than special schools, in the area.
- For children under two, educational provision of any kind.

This is both helpful and unhelpful. It can be seen as helpful in that it clarifies that the way a learning difficulty is perceived has something to do with age-related comparisons between children, and the effective use of educational resources. It can be seen as unhelpful as it is rather bland and does not convey the complexities of the intensity, duration and impact of a disability.

Impairment and disability

Although the two terms 'disability' and 'impairment' are often used together, there are very important differences between the two. This may be best illustrated with a story about Joel. Joel is four years old and is visual impaired. His vision is extremely restricted and, although he can cope quite well when looking at toys very close within his personal space, he finds it very difficult to relate to anything at a greater distance. Joel has a significant visual impairment, which dramatically affects how he relates to his environment. The nature and extent of Joel's impairment cause him to be disabled. However, it can also be argued that society can cause him to be disabled, since if a pair of glasses is available for him, the disabling effect of the impairment is reduced tremendously. If society is unable to supply those glasses, society is contributing to Joel's disability. In many other scenarios, society likewise contributes to the creation of disability. Another story concerns Sarah, a five-year-old girl who was in a car accident. She now has no feeling in her legs. Sarah has a physical impairment that affects her ability to move in her environment, thus disabling her. However, give Sarah a wheelchair, preferably a 'wowee zowee' electric one, and the disability would be greatly reduced.

Impairment then seems to be about something that exists within the person. Impairment is very person-orientated. The child has a particular impairment: physical, emotional, sensory, cognitive. Disability seems then to relate to the impact of the impairment on the experience of the child in the community. Disability is a much more fluid term and can be affected by factors outside of the child and within the community. The availability or, more importantly, the non-availability of services such as glasses, wheelchairs or access to people with appropriate understanding and skills, is a critical part of the equation. The community is an integral part of the whole scenario and can have a great influence on the nature and extent of a disability. The situation is indeed very complex. Let us think about another little boy, Tom, who is also five years old, has social communication difficulties, and exhibits bouts of extreme behaviour. He presents a challenge to staff in his school. We cannot give Tom a pair of glasses or a wheelchair in order to influence and reduce the disabling impact of his impairment. We struggle to try to understand Tom, and in our struggle, the disabling impact of his impairment grows and grows. We need to enable Tom to develop understanding, knowledge and skills that will ultimately impact on the disabling impact of his social communication skills. Tom needs us to understand him. Tom needs us to appreciate what helps him and to facilitate this with him in the community. This requires us to invest in our own knowledge and skills, not just about the impairment, but also about how we can best learn from our children what works well for them, and then to help make this happen with them. Unfortunately, it seems that the current emphasis on knowledge and skills appears to be too closely linked to the impairment of the child, rather than the disability exacerbated by the community. This is illustrated in the recent classification by the Department for Education and Science.

Categories of special educational needs

More recently the DfES has adopted a categorical approach to how learning difficulties are classified:

1. Specific Learning Difficulty (SpLD).
2. Moderate Learning Difficulty (MLD).
3. Severe Learning Difficulty (SLD).
4. Profound and Multiple Learning Difficulty (PMLD).
5. Emotional and Behavioural Difficulty (EBD).
6. Speech, Language and Communication Need (SLCN).
7. Hearing Impairment (HI).
8. Visual Impairment (VI).

9. Multi-sensory Impairment (MSI).
10. Physical Difficulty (PD).
11. Autism Spectrum Disorder (ASD).
12. Other (OTH).

These categories are being used as an audit tool for the Department, and more information about each category can be found on their website (www.DfES.gov.uk). Although they offer clear, simple descriptions about how the government sees a learning difficulty, there is an emphasis on a categorical approach that applies a deficit model to how a child is seen and little recognition of the impact of the community and society on the disabling impact of the categories. The above categories are intended to be used by schools in conjunction with the *Code of Practice* to allocate children to appropriate resource-led categories of provision in school.

The curriculum in the early years

The Foundation Stage, characterized by the Early Learning Goals, forms the central focus of the early years curriculum. Early Learning Goals relate to six areas of development and are described as expectations for the end of the Foundation Stage.

Personal, Social and Emotional Development

By the end of the Foundation stage, most children will:

- continue to be interested, excited and motivated to learn;
- be confident to try new activities, initiate ideas and speak in a familiar group;
- maintain attention, concentrate and sit quietly when appropriate;
- have a developing awareness of their own needs, views and feelings and be sensitive to the needs, views and feelings of others;
- have a developing respect for their own cultures and beliefs and those of other people;
- respond to significant experiences, showing a range of feelings when appropriate;
- form good relationships with adults and peers;
- work as part of a group or class, taking turns and sharing fairly, understanding that there need to be agreed values and codes of behaviour for groups of people, including adults and children, to work together harmoniously;
- understand what is right, what is wrong, and why;
- dress and undress independently and manage their own personal hygiene;
- select and use activities and resources independently;
- consider the consequences of their words and actions for themselves and others;
- understand that people have different needs, views, cultures and beliefs, which need to be treated with respect;

- understand that they can expect others to treat their needs, views, cultures and beliefs with respect.

Communication, Language and Literacy

By the end of the Foundation stage, most children will:

- enjoy listening to and using spoken and written language, and readily turn to it in their play and learning;
- explore and experiment with sounds, words and texts;
- listen with enjoyment and respond to stories, songs and other music, rhymes and poems and make up their own stories, songs, rhymes and poems;
- use language to imagine and recreate roles and experiences;
- use talk to organise, sequence and clarify thinking, ideas, feelings and events;
- sustain attentive listening, responding to what they have heard by relevant comments, questions or actions;
- interact with others, negotiating plans and activities and taking turns in conversation;
- extend their vocabulary, exploring the meanings and sounds of new words;
- retell narratives in the correct sequence, drawing on the language patterns of stories;
- speak clearly and audibly with confidence and control and show awareness of the listener, for example by their use of conventions such as greetings, 'Please' and 'Thank you';
- hear and say initial and final sounds in words, and short vowel sounds within words;
- link sounds to letters, naming and sounding the letters of the alphabet;
- read a range of familiar and common words and simple sentences independently;
- know that print carries meaning and, in English, is read from left to right and top to bottom;
- show an understanding of the elements of stories, such as main character, sequence of events and openings, and how information can be found in non-fiction texts to answer questions about where, who, why and how;
- attempt writing for various purposes, using features of different forms such as lists, stories and instructions;
- write their own names and other things such as labels and captions and begin to form simple sentences, sometimes using punctuation;
- use their phonic knowledge to write simple regular words and make phonetically plausible attempts at more complex words;
- use a pencil and hold it effectively to form recognisable letters, most of which are correctly formed.

Mathematical Development

By the end of the Foundation stage, most children will be able to:

- say and use number names in order in familiar contexts;
- count reliably up to ten everyday objects;
- recognise numerals 1 to 9;
- use language such as 'more' or 'less', 'greater' or 'smaller', 'heavier' or 'lighter', to compare two numbers or quantities;
- in practical activities and discussion begin to use the vocabulary involved in adding and subtracting;
- find one more or one less than a number from 1 to 10;
- begin to relate addition to combining two groups of objects, and subtraction to 'taking away';
- talk about, recognise and recreate simple patterns;
- use language such as 'circle' or 'bigger' to describe the shape and size of solids and flat shapes;
- use everyday words to describe position;
- use developing mathematical ideas and methods to solve practical problems.

Knowledge and Understanding of the World

By the end of the Foundation stage, most children will be able to:

- investigate objects and materials by using all of their senses as appropriate;
- find out about, and identify some features of, living things, objects and events they observe;
- look closely at similarities, differences, patterns and change;
- ask questions about why things happen and how things work;
- build and construct with a wide range of objects, selecting appropriate resources, and adapting their work where necessary;
- select the tools and techniques they need to shape, assemble and join the materials they are using;
- find out about and identify the uses of everyday technology and use information and communication technology and programmable toys to support their learning;
- find out about past and present events in their own lives, and in those of their families and other people they know;
- observe, find out about and identify features in the place in which they live and in the natural world;
- begin to know about their own cultures and beliefs and those of other people;
- find out about their environment, and talk about those features they like and dislike.

Physical Development

By the end of the Foundation stage, most children will be able to:

- move with confidence, imagination and in safety;
- move with control and co-ordination;
- show awareness of space, of themselves and of others;
- recognise the importance of keeping healthy and those things which contribute to this;
- recognise the changes that happen to their bodies when they are active;
- use a range of small and large equipment;
- travel around, under, over and through balancing and climbing equipment;
- handle tools, objects, construction and malleable materials safely and with increasing control.

Creative Development

By the end of the Foundation stage, most children will be able to:

- explore colour, texture, shape, form and space in two and three dimensions;
- recognise and explore how sounds can be changed, sing simple songs from memory, recognise repeated sounds and sound patterns, and match movements to music;
- respond in a variety of ways to what they see, hear, smell, touch and feel;
- use their imagination in art and design, music, dance, imaginative and role play and stories;
- express and communicate their ideas, thoughts and feelings by using a widening range of materials, suitable tools, imaginative and role play, movement, designing and making, and a variety of songs and musical instruments.

The nature of the curriculum in the early years is seen to be a factor conducive to inclusive practice (O'Brien, 2002). The focus on developmentally appropriate skills related to the holistic development of the child in a setting that balances child-initiated with adult-initiated activities is a possible reason for this (Pascal and Bertram, 2001). The flexible, child-centred focus of early years provision offers a nurturing context for learning that should indeed lend itself to meeting a diverse range of learning needs. One of the concerns of the early years curriculum becoming more formalised (and potentially rigid) is that the flexibility that it once had, which is such a conduit for greater inclusive practice, is potentially reduced and may offer greater challenges to the development of greater inclusive practice.

Inclusion in the early years

Early Years Development and Childcare Partnerships (EYDCP) have a remit to meet government targets for the delivery of good quality affordable childcare for 0–14-year-olds, and good quality free early education for all four-year-olds, and for 66 per cent of three-year-olds. An EYDCP represents a wide range of professionals, providers and users of children's services and activities to support parents. Members are drawn from private, public and voluntary sectors. The Partnership itself does not run services or activities, it has a limited number of workers, and limited additional finances to resource new or existing work. The strategic principles that govern the development of early years services are reflected in an EYDCP plan.

The drive for greater inclusion in the early years is evident in both policy and research. The *SEN Code of Practice* (DfES, 2001a) acknowledges that there will be groups of children in the Foundation Stage (three years to end of Reception) that will require support, some of a preventative nature, to have their individual needs met. This is repeated in the National Childcare Standards that state the need: 'To organise the environment and plan activities to ensure that all children take part at a level appropriate to their needs' (Standard Ten DfES, 2001, p. 43).

This is given a level of authority as Ofsted inspect childcare settings in relation to these standards. The positive relationship between the measurement of quality services to diverse early childcare provision is apparent in the literature (Baglin and Bender, 1994; Moss and Pence, 1994). There is a growing interest in the theoretical and practical issues of inclusion in the early years (Wolfendale, 2000; Mittler, 2000; Odom *et al.*, 2000). Inclusion in the early years is seen as beneficial for all children: 'Early intervention techniques developed for children with special needs are useful in enhancing the development of *all* children' (O'Brien, 2002, p. 2). The value of early intervention is well established (Carpenter *et al.*, 1996) as an effective way of meeting the diverse needs of young disabled children. However, an holistic intervention that encompasses health, social care and education is a process that has been difficult to realise in practice (Mittler, 2000). The many variables in service provision are a challenge to co-ordinate into a cohesive single service. However, in the USA, early years inclusive projects that are located in community-based programmes have been seen to be particularly effective (Odom *et al.*, 2000).

Models of organisation in the early years

Models of organisation clearly have relevance to the development of inclusive practice. The systems that we set up can either help or hinder the process of developing greater inclusive practice. The systems can be seen to have different parts and stages:

- immediate to the classroom or setting;
- local to the school or service;
- regional to the area;
- national to the country.

At each of these levels forces come into play that impact upon the quality of the inclusive services we develop, and it is important that we consider issues at each of these levels. McQuail and Pugh (1995) show that some of the key issues relating to effective organisation in the early years are the development of strategic planning, effective resources, evaluation and ownership. It has also been shown that these are factors that may be involved in the effective development of inclusive practice (Dickens and Denziloe, 1998). However, historically involving children with special educational needs in the early years has been problematic and fragmented at national and regional levels (Wolfendale, 2000). There is a great range of varied services involved with young children with special educational needs, and the interaction between these services has often been found wanting. In recent years there have been significant developments in the area of early years organisation. The National Childcare Strategy of 1998 was a direct expression of the commitment of the government to the development of improved provision. The important relationship between early years and special educational needs (DfEE, 1998a) was also highlighted as an area of commitment and concern.

The regional implications of the National Childcare Strategy have been great. The current research of Osgood and Sharp (2000) discusses the organisational structures that local authorities are developing and points to three main models of organisation: co-ordinated, integrated and collaborative. 'Co-ordinated' is where, in an authority, there are discrete departments and services that carry responsibility for early years policy, provision and practice, but are co-ordinated through a formalised structure. This was the most popular model adopted by local authorities. 'Integrated' is where a single department or service holds responsibility for early years in that authority. 'Collaborative' is where officers, with clear lines of demarcation, work in separate departments and early years issues are managed by an Early Years Co-ordinator who liaises between departments. The research evaluated the effectiveness of the different models and found that: 'The more integrated and co-ordinated the early years service was, the more streamlined and focused the provision was seen to be . . . and a more coherent service was seen to be delivered' (Osgood and Sharp, 2000, p. v). It is important to consider the co-ordination and integration of processes at each of the levels outlined at the beginning of this section.

CONCLUSION

This chapter began by discussing how children with special educational needs are described and defined. The underlying tendency to classify children has been discussed as problematic, particularly so when the reality of such classifications is resource-driven. However, classification appears to be here to stay, but does not appear to recognise the complexities, the strengths or disabling impact of the community on a child's special educational need. The curriculum of the early years is described, and it is pointed out that such a curriculum lends itself to inclusive practice. However, further formalization would put this facilitation at risk. The chapter ends by looking at models of early years organisation and how these may best support the development of further inclusive practice. It is shown that the more integrated and co-ordinated the service of early years is, the more coherent the service. Clearly, developing greater collaborative services in the early years is a complex process that demands high levels of cohesion and co-ordination.

CHAPTER 4

'Jungle Journeys' at Summerfield Glade School

The school

Summerfield Glade School is a maintained day special school for boys and girls aged between three and nineteen. The majority of pupils have severe learning difficulties, some with very complex needs, and an increasing number of young pupils with autistic spectrum disorder (ASD). Currently there are 38 pupils on roll and this is steadily increasing. In addition there are eight pupils who are dual registered. All pupils have Statements of Special Educational Needs. The school is in a rural county of the north east of England and some pupils make quite long journeys to school each day. Six pupils are eligible for free school meals. The school is developing very good links with a number of mainstream schools, giving advice and support to a number of pupils with Statements. Some of these pupils are dual registered and spend some sessions in Summerfield Glade School. In addition, a small number of pupils are included in the local middle school for specific subjects. The school receives support and additional finance from the LEA for this work.

In a recent Ofsted inspection Summerfield Glade School was deemed to be an effective school with a number of strengths. The leadership and management of the school by the head teacher was noted as being very good, with him being well supported by a very able deputy head and other key staff who have management responsibilities. Teaching was highlighted as good overall, which results in good learning opportunities for pupils. The teamwork that exists between teachers and teaching assistants was seen as a strength of the school. Pupil achievements are judged to be in line with pupils' abilities, because adults know the pupils well and Individual Education Plans (IEPs) are well targeted to allow pupils to make progress. Young pupils with autistic spectrum disorder were seen to make very good progress in lessons. At Summerfield Glade the intention is to provide a welcoming, supportive environment for pupils and for staff, where good communications with the pupils, their guardians, visitors and the wider community of professionals are fostered. To this end, the school's aims are to:

- provide every pupil with a broad and balanced curriculum that meets his or her cultural, physical, social, spiritual, moral and emotional needs within the framework of the National Curriculum;
- provide a range of activities suitable to age and ability to ensure that each pupil learns at an appropriate pace;
- provide clear behavioural boundaries and guidelines for all pupils;
- ensure equality of access to the curriculum, regardless of the degree of a pupil's disability, their gender, race or culture;
- equip each pupil with the necessary concepts, attitudes, skills and knowledge for life in the wider community;
- foster enthusiastic, positive, lively, enquiring pupils, respectful of and sensitive to the needs of other people, where all are treated with dignity.

The class

Class 1 has nine full-time and two part-time pupils. It is a mixed Reception and Year 1 class.

Children enjoying the story in Summerfield Glade School

The adults

Mrs S., the teacher, qualified as a teacher of pupils with severe learning difficulties in 1980 after studying for four years at CF Mott College in Liverpool. She taught for three years at a college in Liverpool for pupils aged sixteen to nineteen, then moved to another teaching position at an all-age special school for pupils with SLD. She stayed at this school for thirteen years. Some of this time was part-time and included maternity leave and a two-year break. She started at Summerfield Glade School in 1996, returning to the north east for family reasons and her husband's job. She initially taught part-time in the Reception class but now teaches full-time in both the Reception class and Key Stage 2. She is the senior teacher with responsibility for the primary department, inclusion and mathematics. The school receives extra funding to support inclusion work with local mainstream schools, and Mrs S. manages this. There are currently eight pupils dual registered between Summerfield Glade and their local mainstream school. Mrs S. is married to a head teacher and has three children aged seventeen, fifteen and twelve.

Mrs C., the classroom assistant, followed a BEd. Hons degree course and was awarded a Diploma of Higher Education, having followed an approved route in Primary Education. She is a registered child minder and has completed a preparation course for 'Sponsored Daycare', a Certificate of Awareness in Caring for Children with HIV and a First Aid certificate for an appointed person in a county school.

'Walking through the jungle . . . what do you see? . . . over there . . . a lion looking for his tea'

Mrs N., classroom assistant, usually works in another class. However, during this lesson, she was covering for a staff member. Mrs N. became a parent helper in classes when her own two children started school in Brussels. She then started work in the school's kinder crib, covering maternity leave. Since moving back to England, she has completed the NCFE Classroom Assistant, Stage 1, started working at the Summerfield Glade School, and has just received funding to commence the NVQ Level 3 in Early Years Childcare and Education.

Mrs M., the nursery nurse, started at Summerfield Glade when she was sixteen years old on a Youth Training Scheme, in early years. After leaving to start a family, Mrs M. returned part-time in 1999, working one-to-one with a child. She is now a full-time nursery nurse working in Class 1, with Reception and Year 1 children.

The children

Laura has attended Summerfield Glade School full-time since September 2002. She has global developmental delay in all areas. She has difficulty in maintaining attention and needs to work on an individual basis for short focused learning tasks, with consolidation of skills and general activities taking place in the group setting. Laura currently needs close supervision at all times, as she has no sense of danger and can behave inappropriately towards other pupils. Laura is learning to follow instructions at the two information word carrying level. She needs support to follow general requests in the classroom and is using a PECS approach to help focus her communication skills. Laura has a wide vocabulary but many of the phrases she uses are 'learned' phrases rather than spontaneous communication.

From her extensive IEP her Language and Literacy targets are that she will:

- follow requests with two key words. The criterion for success is that she will follow the request in home or doll play using an action and object (P level 5);
- have the opportunity to develop her reading skills through reading her own photograph-based books with pictures of her family and friends. Laura will be encouraged to locate named photographs by pointing. Laura will be given the opportunity to listen to familiar rhymes and stories, and look at books herself;
- be encouraged to use books appropriately, turning the pages and holding the book the right way up;
- use a symbol-based timetable and be encouraged to recognise symbols in object-, picture- or symbol-matching activities;
- recognise her own name and those of her class peers;
- match objects to symbols. Laura will place the object on the symbol from a choice of three (P level 5);
- be encouraged to make marks with a variety of materials, such as chalks, crayons or felt pens alongside a picture;

- be encouraged to place photographs and symbols on a personal timetable.
- have opportunities to use the PC, to generate a symbol from a selection on the computer, and then make marks using a paint program.

In relation to her social development, Laura usually co-operates with adult requests given on an individual basis in the classroom. She knows the names of all her peers in Class 1 and of a number of staff. She gives eye contact appropriately, but needs to develop her attention skills. Laura has a behaviour management plan. She is able to drink using a normal cup. She can pick up and put down her cup on the table appropriately. She is learning to pour her own drink. She is using the PECS system to indicate choices during snack time. Laura is able to eat her dinner independently using a spoon and a mannoy dish. She is to be encouraged to stab at food using a fork and to refrain from using her fingers. She is able to make a choice of dessert, and is regularly given the opportunity to do so. Laura needs to learn how to eat foods such as sandwiches appropriately, taking small bites.

Her Personal, Social and Health Education targets are to:

- follow a toilet training programme in school and at home under the direction of the community nurse;
- be encouraged to dress and undress as independently as possible;
- use a fork to stab her food. Laura will hold the fork in her right hand and stab at foods such as chips, fish fingers, etc. She will hold a spoon in her left hand and refrain from putting her fingers in her dinner.

Andrew attends a local First School for two afternoons with additional support. At Summerfield Glade School he is in Class 1 where he is a member of a class of five full-time and four part-time pupils. Andrew has general learning difficulties, with specific difficulties in expressive language. He is developing a range of approximations to spoken words and uses a number of symbols for communication. He does not spontaneously sign, but Makaton and symbols are being used daily and encouraged.

Andrew's efforts at making himself both heard and understood have developed significantly recently. He has developed a motivation to use his voice, and his symbol recognition is developing well, now being able to use two symbols, in a structured setting, for example, 'I want' + 'crisps'. Andrew is encouraged to attempt to use words appropriately in conjunction with symbols, and Makaton signing as appropriate during the school day.

Andrew has been participating in an oro-motor session on a weekly basis with the speech therapists. He enjoys regular literacy lessons based around simple fiction. He understands the conventions of reading a book – left to right, top to bottom, and page following page. He is interested in the text and in the activity of reading. He enjoys making marks using various implements. He needs opportunities to develop a pincer grasp and to use more pressure when mark-making. He understands that print carries meaning and will scribble alongside a picture.

From his extensive IEP, Andrew's Language and Literacy targets are that he will:

- recognise all relevant timetable symbols and will select a verbally requested symbol from a choice of four each time;
- match letters and short (story related) words;
- select and recognise names of class peers;
- predict words in a familiar story when the adult stops reading;
- make choices between symbols and pictures in the context of text by selecting pictures or symbols to show what is represented in a story. The selection will include symbols and pictures unrelated to the text;
- use squeezy scissors to cut paper;
- colour within lines;
- trace over shapes and letters.

In relation to his social development, Andrew requires some support for dressing and undressing for PE. He requires prompts for hand washing. A community health nurse has investigated a toileting programme, although it appears from baseline recording that Andrew is still unready for toilet training. Andrew can now use a knife and fork correctly at lunchtimes and can make a drink of juice with only a little supervision. More recently, Andrew has developed a desire to express his needs and wants. These are sometimes expressed to the adults he works with, but mainly to the pupils he plays with most in his class. He enjoys a range of play with a variety of toys and particularly enjoys simple interactive games with a peer, such as a chasing game. His attendance at his local First School for two afternoons each week provides opportunities for interacting socially with mainstream pupils in his local school community. The specific target for this integration is:

- Andrew will take turns in a tabletop activity with peers. Adult prompts will initially be given for Andrew to understand when it is his turn in a group of three or four pupils. The support will be withdrawn as Andrew's awareness increases.

Katy is in her Reception year at Summerfield Glade School. Katy communicates through facial expression, body language and vocalisations. A single word, 'Mummy', has been heard once recently in school. During the last half-term, Katy has responded well to the adults in her environment and also, to a lesser extent, to her peers. She prefers interaction with adults, and has shown a preference for a particular member of staff when working.

Katy shows selective attention to learning situations, and needs to be involved in routines and learning opportunities with adult support. Her attention can be of short duration and she does not yet maintain eye contact for prolonged periods of time to enable shared attention to tasks. In Literacy, Katy is encouraged to attend to stories that are supported with items relating to the narrative. Katy is beginning to imitate some basic Makaton signs that relate to routines in the classroom, for example, she can imitate the response 'Yes' when her name is called at registration time. She has recently shown an interest in the timetables of the other pupils in Class 1; therefore a photographic timetable will be developed and introduced at a rate that enables Katy's participation and success. She will also be introduced to PECS, where a picture is exchanged for an item as a form of communication.

From her extensive IEP, Katy's Language and Literacy targets are to:

- exchange a photograph for a drink, snack, sand play and doll play. Photographs of two of the four above will be presented, and Katy will indicate her choice by giving her chosen item or activity photo to the adult;
- eye-point to pupils and staff. Katy will match photos of the staff members to give her diary to in circle time and make a choice from photos of two peers as to who she wishes to play with. Handing the photo to the adult will demonstrate this choice.

In relation to her social development, Katy is given opportunities to develop awareness of herself through a range of activities, including PE for body awareness, choice-making for emotional development and play for social development. Katy still requires adult support to make choices and does not have many strong preferences that are expressed, other than enjoying other people doing things for her! She is, however, encouraged to do anything she possibly can, given adult support. Katy drinks small amounts of juice or milk from a two-handled cup with an easy-sip lid. Her food is either chopped small, or liquidised to a coarse texture, since she is reluctant to chew her food. Her feeding skills are being overseen by the speech therapists. Katy needs adult help with dressing and undressing for PE. She does not enjoy this, but is encouraged to participate with pulling off easy items of clothing. Katy wears nappies at school and relies on adults for all her toileting needs. She shows no awareness of when soiled or wet. She enjoys the daily Circle Time, where she is supported with activities such as responding to her name being called, finding her photograph to put on the board and having her home news read. She also learns to relate to others in her group by looking at, and touching, the pupil next to her in the circle after she has had her turn. Katy has opportunities to interact with pupils from a local nursery each week. Her Personal, Social and Health Education target is:

- Katy will feed herself using a spoon, with gradual increases in food texture.

Peter is in his Reception year. He commenced attendance at Summerfield Glade School on a part-time basis in September 2001, moving towards full-time attendance in January 2002. Peter has significant language and communication delay due to Autistic Spectrum Disorder. Peter is encouraged to listen and respond to routines and activities in class.

He makes some repetitive speech sound patterns, which can disrupt his attention; staff discourage these, and active listening is encouraged. Some of Peter's speech and language is immature and idiosyncratic; the speech therapists are currently working on an assessment of his linguistic abilities. At present, he is responding to simple verbal requests and instructions, and can use words to name items and express immediate needs. Phrases are heard but are context- and situation-dependent. Peter enjoys story time and responds well to books and also to the pictures and symbols that accompany them. He knows some letter sounds, but is unable to break words down or identify initial sounds in words. He can identify his written name.

From his extensive IEP, Peter's Language and Literacy targets are to:

- extend his Subject-Verb-Object structures by discussing three sequential pictures. He will sequence three pictures correctly and answer questions on the story line;
- read the following key words. I/is/and/he/are/the/a/to/she/at/. Initially the words will be highlighted in context, within texts, and gradually will be presented out of context for him to recognise;
- practise independent formation and sequencing of the letters of his first name.

In relation to social development, Peter's social interactions are clearly affected by his autism. He can name his peers in Class 1, and is beginning to migrate towards them when observing their play in the playground. He enjoys watching their fun but does not join in. Peter has regular weekly opportunities to become involved in play activities with pupils from a local nursery. Peter eats a limited range of foods and is reluctant to use cutlery. He will drink at present from only one beaker at home. Peter attends to his own toileting needs and is able to dress and undress himself with help from an adult for fastenings. His Personal, Social and Health Education target is:

- He will accept drinking from a cup at home and at school.

Philip is in National Curriculum Year 1. Philip has learnt to use symbols for a range of words and activities related to the school day. He has increased his amount of spoken language through the reading of such symbols, and also by learning and being encouraged to participate in routines throughout the school day. Philip tends to be quiet and undemanding, yet can enter into activities he enjoys, showing a greater expanse of language. The speech and language therapists attached to the school are advising about Philip's targets. He has responded well to the structure, routine and use of symbols used in Class 1. He is interested in the familiar adults and peers around him and can name them all. His spoken language still tends to be used only in situations that require a response, for example, asking for a snack at break time. He does not yet initiate communication and requires prompting from an adult. He has participated in listening to stories that are supported by objects and symbols to aid understanding. He can respond appropriately to simple questions of the 'What is this?' type, using one-word responses. Philip is recognising that words relate to people, situations, actions and objects. Already he is consistently recognising all his class peers and relating them to photographs too. He understands the conventions of a reading book very well, for example, front page significance, left to right, top and bottom. Philip is predominantly right-handed. He can track lines from right to left and will develop this skill further through the use of handwriting development sheets.

From his extensive IEP Philip's Language and Literacy targets are to:

- place an item in the correct position stated by the adult, given a choice of two toys and two possible targets for the placement, e.g., put the <u>teddy</u> <u>under</u> the <u>bed</u>;
- discriminate between initial phonemes in initial place in listening games. By playing the jingles game, he will match an object to the initial sound he hears;
- develop a pincer grasp through using small pieces of chalk or pencil.

In relation to his social development, Philip can dress and undress himself, needing some help with the orientation of clothing, fastenings, and shoes and socks. He has learnt to make, and pour, a drink at snack time, but often hesitates and prefers an adult to be on hand to give a little guidance. He wears nappies at school and at home. He has become more willing to eat a range of foods, and eats many of the school dinners provided. His weight is still monitored by the school nurse. Although Philip has a great interest in his peers and the adults with whom he works, he remains a relatively solitary and undemanding boy. He does, however, learn to carry out new tasks, such as taking the register to the office, with no sign of anxiety. Philip is beginning to make simple requests from the adults around him when he needs help. He enjoys watching other children at play, and plays alongside or follows them. Philip has opportunities to interact with children who come from a local nursery every Tuesday afternoon. He does not relate to the other children, but will play quite happily alongside them. His Personal, Social and Health Education target is:

- He will request the continuation of an enjoyable experience. An adult will initiate a game for two pupils, involving Philip. Philip will ask for 'More' or 'Again', and the adult will withdraw as progress is made.

The planning

Long-term planning

See Table 4.1.

Table 4.1 Summerfield Glade School National Literacy Strategy (Summer Term 2003)

Class 1
Teacher/Support staff: Mrs S., Mrs N. and Ms C.

Text/Range	Speaking and Listening
Fiction: familiar repetitive rhymes. Poetry: rhymes. Non-fiction: bubbles linked to science theme.	Be able to recount main points of a story. Develop auditory discrimination skills. Recognise storybook language. Understand and use nouns, verbs, adjectives at two-, three-, four-word level. Begin to respond consistently to familiar people, events and objects. Begin to communicate intentionally.

Reading
Learn key words.
Match letters to sounds.
Recognise familiar words in a text.
Focus attention on certain people, events or objects.
Match symbols to objects/words.
Accept and engage in coactive exploration, focusing attention on sensory aspects of stories.

Writing
Take part in shared writing using names of pupils in class.
Recount main parts of story using pictures/symbols or words.
Practise correct letter formation.
Use symbols for writing.
Actively manipulate objects: grasp and release, open and close hands.
Imitate scribbling marks on paper or other surface.

Medium-term planning

See Table 4.2.

Table 4.2 National Literacy Strategy (Summer Term 2003)

Individual Learning Targets

Date and text title	Speaking and Listening	Reading	Writing
2/6/03 *Peace at Last*	**Laura** will follow requests with two key words.	**Laura** will match objects to symbols.	**Peter** will hold his pencil with correct grip.
9/6/03 *Walking Through the Jungle*	**Andrew** will clap syllables related to words.	**Andrew** will match ten words to symbols that relate to his timetable.	**Andrew** will accurately trace over curved line patterns.
16/6/03 *Row Your Boat*	**Katy** will exchange a symbol for a desired object.	**Katy** will eye-point to pupils and staff.	**Philip** will form the letters t and h correctly.
23/6/03 *Lofty Visits the Farm*	**Peter** will develop the use of pronouns he, she and they.	**Peter** will read a minimum of twelve words from the literacy strategy list of high-frequency words.	**Laura** will copy straight lines and circles in mark-making.
30/6/03 *Lofty Visits the Seaside*	**Philip** will use verbs at the two-word level to describe picture materials.	**Philip** will match initial phenomes with graphemes in words.	**Katy** will use a range of materials – chalk, pencils, finger paint – to make marks on paper.
7/7/03 *Bubbles*			

Laura and Amy drawing over their crocodiles

Short-term planning

Aims for the lesson

The lesson is based on the story book *Walking Through the Jungle*.

Learning Outcome Focus: Speaking and Listening
- All pupils will listen to and respond to animal sounds linked to the story.
- Most pupils will recognise and name animals linked to the text.
- Few pupils will respond to three-word level requests using objects related to the text.

Learning Outcome Focus: Reading
- All pupils will look at objects, pictures or symbols that relate to text.
- Most pupils will match objects to pictures and symbols.
- Few pupils will match letters to build words.

Learning Outcome Focus: Writing
- All pupils will move their hands over textures to explore animal coats.
- Most pupils will make marks with paint using brushes and sponges.
- Few pupils will trace over an outline of animals linked to text with accuracy.

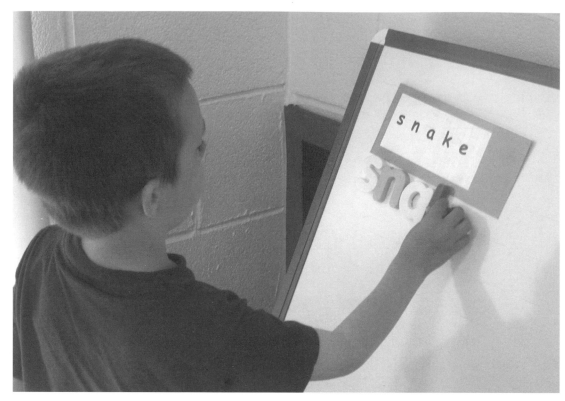

Peter finding the letters to spell 'snake'

The lesson

Monday

Whole class activity
- Read *Walking Through the Jungle*, emphasizing high-interest words (animal names).
- Use three repetitive phrases of 'walking through the jungle', 'What do you see?' and 'I see an . . . looking for his tea'.

Guided task
- Match animals to symbols.

Individual and small group work
- Group 1: Peter, Philip and Andrew to attempt initial letter sounds worksheet, final sounds for Peter.
- Group 2: Laura to match animals activity and sort animals from food items. Katy to activate Big Mack to listen to animal sounds.

Plenary

- Recall sequence of animals in the book using symbols with text as a prompt.

Tuesday

Whole class activity

- Read story and encourage children to join in with repetitive phrases.

Guided task

- Make appropriate animal sound to picture or symbol.

Individual and small group work

- Group 1: Peter, Philip, Andrew to attempt letter-matching activity and word-matching worksheet.
- Group 2: Laura and Katy to follow a trail around school to find hidden animals.

Plenary

- Group 2 to show and name the animals found on the trail.

Thursday

Whole class activity

- Re-read story and pause to see if pupils can complete repetitive phrases, locating animals hidden around classroom as story is read.

Guided task

- Find named symbols of animals. Flashcards introduced.

Individual and small group work

- Group 1: Peter, Philip and Andrew to read flashcards of animal names. Spell animal names using magnetic letters.
- Group 2: Laura and Katy to make animal masks.

Plenary

- Group 1 to lay out animal pictures and show pupils matching flashcards. To be encouraged to read cards then find matching picture.

Peter's successful 'snake' word

Evaluation

The adults involved in the lesson collectively reflected on how the lesson had gone. During the whole class activity there was excellent attention given to story. Most pupils could actively search for their given animal, the less able fixated and tracked the movement of a toy animal. Future ideas could potentially include more use of animal sounds with toy animals out of sight and pupils having to listen to locate them. Group 1 pupils were both able to match letters to build words. Peter was able to read all the animal names. Philip was able to read 'elephant'. Both children seemed to enjoy the task and were actively involved for the duration of the activity. In Group 2, Laura completed her matching and sorting activities successfully. She completed animal matching silhouette worksheet independently. The adults felt that, to increase the challenge for this group, they could have moved on to a more challenging activity at this point. For example, to increase their scanning and identifying strategies, they could match animal silhouette shapes from a more jumbled array of animal and other shapes. Katy made appropriate use of the Big Mac, and her attention to the crocodile task was good. Group 1 participated in the flashcard and magnetic letter activities, adult prompts being needed to support word recognition, for example, focusing on initial letter sounds. Both Laura and Katy had high motivation for the school trail where they were actively searching for the animal puppets around the school. Laura and Katy required constant adult support in order to complete this activity. Groups 1 and 2 participated well in the plenary. Philip, Andrew and Peter led the involvement in the recall sequence of animals in the book, and Katy and Laura showed the animals they found on their school trail. The trail around class was a huge success where the children displayed high motivation and all participated in locating the animals. Mrs C., one of the teaching assistants, informed Mrs S., the teacher, about Philip's word recognition so she could target a successful response from him in the plenary, allowing him to finish positively.

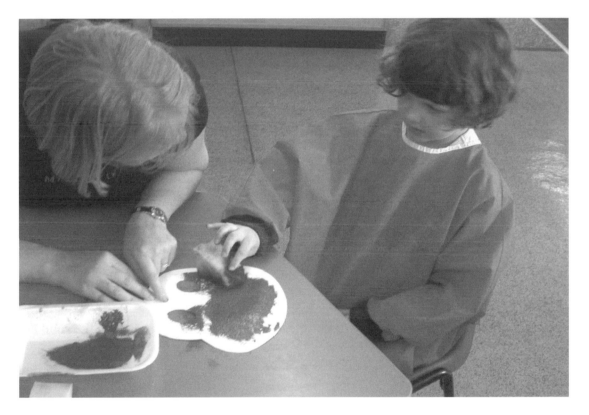

Laura making her monkey mask

CHAPTER 5

'Musical Melodies' at Springfield First School

The school

Springfield First School is situated in the village of Snow Town, a rural village in Northumberland. The first school was built in 1697 and extensively modernised in 1911. It derives its name from the Reverend John Springfield. The school receives grants from the Springfield Educational Foundation on a regular basis. Pupils come from a range of backgrounds: many have long-established connections with the village, others have recently moved into the community. A significant number of pupils come from outside the catchment area. There is a nursery unit which offers part-time education to about 50 pupils. Most pupils attend the nursery for three terms prior to their entry to the Reception class at the start of the academic year in which they become five years old. The school aims to serve the needs of every pupil, enabling them to reach their full potential. In their last Ofsted inspection the following statement was written:

> This is a good school with many significant strengths. The head teacher provides good professional leadership, a clear educational direction for the work of the school and is constantly trying to improve the quality of education that the school provides.
> The governors take an active part in school life and provide very good support and encouragement for the school. They are dedicated to providing a high standard of education for all pupils. Together with the staff, they work as a team and are largely successful in meeting the school's aims. Pupils' attitudes and behaviour are good and this has a positive impact on their work and the standards that they attain. The personal development of pupils is effectively managed and, as a result, they show high levels of confidence and self-discipline. This makes a positive contribution to the purposeful, happy learning ethos within the school. Pupils who are under five respond well to the opportunities they are given and enjoy learning. Their behaviour is good and they are gaining in confidence and self-esteem. They relate well to each other, take turns, and share resources.

Children enjoying Music Time at Springfield Nursery

The class

This is a 26-place nursery class where children attend on a part-time basis, mainly mornings. The building is separate from the main school and has a dedicated playground. The children spend some time in the main school for physical education, music and whole school activities and celebrations. The nursery itself is a one-storey building that is open plan in nature. Established activity areas are set up, some of these change depending on the current nursery theme.

The staff

The teacher, Mrs H., has been in post seventeen years and has lived in the village for that length of time too. She holds a Certificate of Education and is well known in the local community. Many of the parents of the children who attend the nursery have known Mrs H. for many years. She enjoys a particular standing in the community. Her nursery

Waiting for turns

nurse, Mrs S., has worked at the school for eight years. She holds a NNEB, nursery nurse qualification, and also lives in the village. Her son attends the nursery and she knows many of the parents and children personally as well as professionally. Other professionals involved with the pupil who is the focus of our interest are the school Special Educational Needs Co-ordinator (SENCO), the Speech and Language Therapist for the area, and staff at the Hearing Impaired Service. His parents also took him to an ENT consultant.

The children

The nursery has a mixed ability intake. The present class has twenty pupils: six girls and fourteen boys. The ambience in the class is physical, with a tendency for the large number of boys to be particularly boisterous. Peter does not have a Statement, but he is on the Action Plus stage of the *Code of Practice*.

Passing the bean-bag

Table 5.1 Peter's Individual Action Plan

School: Springfield First School   **Name:** Peter   **Class/Phase:** Nursery

Date started: January 2003   **Review date:** April 2003

Targets	Strategies, resources and responsibilities
1. I will try not to touch other children.	Social story. Reward system. Use of role models.
2. I will collect my coat and leave without making a fuss.	Reward system. Model desired behaviour. Use of role models.

Date started: May 2003   **Review date:** October 2003

Targets	Strategies, resources and responsibilities
1. Listen to adults and comply with reasonable requests. e.g., Tidy away toys, stand with a partner.	Give child prior warning of request and make expectation clear. Use peers as role models. Praise desired behaviour. Set a suitable sanction that he can understand and relate to undesirable behaviour.

Peter is four years old and has attended the nursery since the previous September. He has hearing, speech and behaviour issues and was taken into care because of child protection issues. His family in the village adopted him when he was two years old and he is an only child. He was still on a milk diet when he came to his adoptive family and had no experience of solid food. He had spent long periods of time strapped in a pushchair upstairs while the adults were elsewhere in the house. Recent investigations regarding hearing loss suggest that there has been some permanent damage. He was not talking when he joined his foster family.

The speech therapist for the area assessed Peter during his first term in the nursery, and her assistant worked with him for two six-week periods. At first he refused to interact with her and would not take part in any of the activities that she tried to introduce. Fortunately there was a second child in the setting who needed her help, and who willingly took part in these sessions. Some of the fun things that they were doing were emphasized to Peter. For example, there were bubble blowing, games and toys that were not available in the classroom. After a couple of sessions, Peter decided that he would join in after all. Through this his attention and concentration levels were gradually extended.

The staff in the class felt that some of Peter's challenging behaviour occurred because he was an excitable child who was not yet in control of his emotions. His challenging behaviours usually related to control issues. Peter often refused to join in with group activities or even to work with one other child. These activities were not particularly difficult; in fact, they were usually fun things that the other children joined in eagerly. He would say, 'I not doing that', and walk or run away from the activity, or would shout out and drop to the ground. Mrs H. could not always be sure when this would happen. Peter was unpredictable. However, when the class went to the main school for their movement lesson, there would invariably be a difficult incident with Peter. The children walked across to school in pairs. Peter always wanted to choose his partner and always wanted to be first to choose. When told it was not his turn that week he always screamed, cried and lay down on the floor. Once in the hall, the children were each given a small plastic basket into which they put their sweaters, shoes and socks. The baskets were in four different colours and they were handed out randomly. No matter what colour basket Peter was given, it was not the colour he wanted! He would then refuse to take off his shoes and socks. School staff were very consistent in expectations, and Peter could not join in the lesson until he removed his footwear. Consequently, he had to sit at the side of the hall until he did.

Peter sometimes complied quickly, sometimes only when he realised that the other children were having fun while he was missing out, while at other times his behaviour deteriorated. On these occasions he would shout in a loud voice that disturbed other classes, try to leave the hall area or push other children. This was when a 'time out' strategy was implemented. Peter was removed to a place where he could neither see, nor be seen by, the rest of the group. There was no verbal interaction while he was being moved. Either the nursery nurse or teacher stayed beside him, with no interaction. This strategy usually had the desired effect. He did not always join in, but he always calmed down and walked back to nursery as if nothing had happened. In general, turn-taking was a problem. Peter did not seem to understand that other children wanted toys and equipment as much as he did, and that everyone could have a turn, but some had to wait a while for that to happen. The wheeled toys (bikes, scooters and trucks) for outdoor play were another particularly difficult area. Peter had a favourite bike and he did not like the other children to have it. If he was playing on the climbing frame or with a ball, he expected that 'his' bike would not be used by others. When he noticed any other child riding on it, he immediately ran across to them and pushed them off.

Throughout his nursery year, staff worked consistently on turn-taking with the class in as many situations as possible and were able to help Peter adapt his behaviour during the year and begin to accept sharing toys, equipment and attention. All of the adults in the nursery liked Peter. He is bubbly and lively. He is quick to notice new displays and activities, and asks lots of 'Why?' and 'What's that for?' questions. He likes to give hugs to the adults. Indeed, he sometimes tried to hug his way out of difficult situations! Some of the more timid children were wary of him and his outbursts. Occasionally he struck out at others when he was particularly upset. Despite this, he was popular with many of the boys, who would choose him as a playmate before others. Peter liked to be helpful. He liked to put a chair ready for an adult at Story Time and sometimes helped to tidy away the toys at the end of the session. Peter enjoyed physical play most of all. He is well co-ordinated and was adept at climbing and swinging from the climbing frame. Indoors he liked the train track (as long as he could have all the trains), construction toys and the computer.

The joy of the triangle

The planning

Long-term planning

Table 5.2 Long-term planning at Springfield School

Long-term plan (Summer Term)			Foundation Stage			
Topic	**Personal, social and emotional development**	**Communication, language and literacy**	**Mathematical development**	**Knowledge and understanding of the world**	**Physical development**	**Creative development**
Rainforest changes	Concentration and perseverance Adapting to new situations	Introduce phonics	Language of shape and size	Patterns in the natural world Construct for a purpose	Throwing, catching and kicking skills	Respond to music with movement.
Growing .	Responsibility and respect Working together	Imaginative use of language Reading comprehension	Abacus scheme	Sense of time: life cycles and growing Exploration and investigation of growing things Summer	Look at different artists Performing	Safely move with confidence and control Handle tools, objects, construction and malleable materials safely and with increasing control
Out and about	Moral and cultural development Sense of community Appropriate behaviour Turn-taking and sharing Concentration and perseverance Working co-operatively	Using reading strategies Independent writing Writing for different purposes Planning and evaluation Communication skills Listening skills Vocabulary development	Language of time and money Mathematical vocabulary One-to-one Correspondence Counting Practical problem-solving, including money	Sense of place Cultures and beliefs ICT – refer to separate plan Vocabulary Cultural celebrations Sense of time Exploration and investigation Construction skills	Printing Patterns in the environment Music from around the world Communicate and evaluate their own and others' work Country dancing Use of imagination in art and design, dance, music	Awareness of themselves, others and space Correct and safe use of equipment Fine motor skills Gross motor skills Confidence Control and co-ordination Vocabulary

Table 5.2 Long-term planning at Springfield School – continued

Long-term plan (Summer Term)		Foundation Stage			
Topic	Personal, social and emotional development	Communication, language and literacy	Mathematical development	Knowledge and understanding of the world	Physical development	Creative development
	Respect for and from others	Reading comprehension				Role-play and stories
	Independence in self-help skills	Reading conventions				Respond, express and communicate ideas, thoughts and feelings in a variety of ways using all the senses
	Effective relationships	Emergent writing				
	Moral development	Literacy in role-play situations				
	Response to cultural, religious events and other significant experiences					Skills and techniques
						Vocabulary
	Respect for others' needs and beliefs					Explore colour, texture, shape, form and space in 2D and 3D
						Safe use of tools

The long-term planning shows the context for the lesson at Springfield First School. It also reflects the shared planning that occurs with the Reception class in the school. This co-ordinated planning occurs in every term of the school year.

Medium-term planning

See Table 5.3.

Short-term planning

See Table 5.4.

The overall aim of the session for all the children was to join in with singing songs and take part in a turn-taking activity. The aim for Peter was to include him in the activity and to show him that he could have a turn, if he joined in the whole activity with the other children.

Table 5.3 Medium-term planning at Springfield School

Medium-term plan (Summer Term)

Personal, social and emotional development	Communication, language and literacy	Mathematical development	Knowledge and understanding of the world	Physical development	Creative development
To be able to stay at a self-chosen activity for increasing periods of time. To begin to express needs and feelings appropriately. To show confidence in linking up with others for support.	To begin to give explanations as to why things happen. To begin to hear and say initial sounds of words. To learn that some books are story books and others give us information.	To be able to recognise and re-create repeating patterns. To begin to use the language of direction. To be able to separate a group of objects in different ways and begin to realise that the total remains the same.	To be able to use a programmable toy. To begin to construct for a purpose. To show curiosity and manipulate objects.	To show an awareness of keeping healthy. To develop throwing and catching skills. To be able to show increasing control when climbing, swinging and scrambling.	To explore materials to make 3D structures. To make pictures using mixed media. To explore the sounds of different instruments.

The lesson

All children and both adults sit in a circle with the following musical instruments in the centre of the circle: tambourine, triangle, maracas, wooden sticks, hand bells, and castanets. A bean-bag is passed around the circle (similar to Pass the Parcel) while everyone sings, 'Choose an instrument you can play, you can play, you can play. Choose an instrument you can play. What's your favourite?' When the song ends, the child holding the bean-bag exchanges it for the instrument of his or her choice. They play their chosen instrument while everyone sings: 'David plays the tambourine, tambourine, tambourine. David plays the tambourine. That's his favourite.' The game has been played before and so the children are familiar with it. It is the first time that the triangle has been included in the selection of instruments being used.

Peter spots the triangle immediately and loudly states, 'I want that.' Mrs H. replies, 'Let's play the game, and you can have a turn.' Peter joins in, but doesn't have the bean-bag when the song ends. He is unhappy, but stays in the circle. The tension is mounting. The child who has the bean-bag chooses the triangle. Peter screams and stamps his feet. He moves himself out of the circle and into a corner of the room. He covers his ears and turns away. Mrs H. approaches him and reiterates to him that if he rejoins the circle and plays the game, he may get a turn. Mrs H. returns to the main group and resumes the

Table 5.4 Weekly plan for Springfield School

Weekly plan (Summer Term, Week 1)

Personal, social and emotional development	Communication, language and literacy	Mathematical development	Knowledge and understanding of the world	Physical development	Creative development
To be able to form good relationships with adults and other children.	To be able to speak out with confidence in a large group.	To be able to count on from a given number less than 6.	To show curiosity and manipulate objects.	To be able to move in a range of ways and with increasing control on apparatus.	To join in singing and use percussion instruments to accompany the songs.
To be able to share activities and equipment with friends.	To have the confidence to talk in a small group.	To be able to say number names in order to 10.	1. To notice and be aware of the collections of objects.	To be able to climb the ladder of the climbing frame.	1. To join in with tapping rhythms when singing.
To be able to include others in the group with adult support.	To have the confidence to speak in a large group with adult support.	To be able to count on when starting with 2 or 3.	2. To look carefully, touch and handle the objects.	To be able to hang from the ladder with adult support.	2. To be able to remember how to hold and play the instruments.
To be able to take turns and share activities and equipment with everyone.	To be able to speak confidently in a large group.	To be able to count on from 2, 3, 4 and 5.	3. To begin to ask questions, talk about and compare the objects.	To be able to climb, hang from and get down from the climbing apparatus independently.	3. To be able to take turns and share the instruments.
Activities. Outdoor toys e.g. bikes, balls. Construction equipment, cars, trains, turn-taking games.	Adult-initiated conversations in small group situations during play leading on to Circle Time sessions in larger groupings.	Whole class, small group or paired work using objects, number lines etc.	Interest table with a variety of collections of natural objects, wind-up toys, magnets, torches.	Adult support and encouragement every day to ensure every child can use the climbing frame with confidence.	Access to music table with selection of percussion instruments, tape recorder and song tapes. Music time session.

game. Peter remains in the corner of the room, sometimes peeping around. Mrs H. and Mrs S. reward the other children in the group, and the activity continues.

After two more rounds, Mrs H. invites Peter to sit with her. He agrees and moves to sit in front of Mrs H. on the carpet. The game carries on. Peter refuses to touch the bean-bag as it moves past him. Mrs H. physically passes the bean-bag across him, waiting for a few seconds to see if Peter will take hold of it. On the next round of the song, Peter reaches for the bean-bag and sings along. Mrs H. offers him non-verbal praise with a beaming smile. Two turns later, the bean-bag stops at Peter when the song ends. He chooses the triangle, sings along and participates enthusiastically, but appropriately.

Evaluation

Mrs H. and Mrs S. both participated in the reflection of the lesson. They felt the activity was clearly highly motivating for all the children, Peter was keen to participate and chose to return to the activity and behave appropriately. The aims for the activity were successfully met for all children. Peter did have a challenging outburst when he became frustrated at having to wait his turn. Mrs H. responded to him in a calm, consistent, but firm manner. She adopted a classroom procedure that was well established in the class, inviting him back in, but reiterating the classroom expectations. Mrs H. had her expectations for the group and made it obvious to Peter that he, too, had to meet those to be part of the activity. She did, however, offer him support strategies to rejoin the group. These included physical proximity to her, and also praise of appropriate behaviour. In this time of stress for Peter, he desperately wanted the bean-bag and triangle, and he wanted them immediately. The well-established classroom procedures helped enormously to bring about the desired outcome. After a short time away, Peter rejoined the group, sitting close to the teacher for support, and successfully completed the activity.

CHAPTER 6

'Fantastic Fruit' at Blackberry Hill School

The school

Blackberry Hill is a purpose-built primary co-educational day school for children with learning difficulties (moderate, severe, profound and multiple). Some of the children also have autism. Blackberry Hill has 96 places for pupils and has a total of 39 staff: a head teacher, deputy head teacher, thirteen teachers and 24 special support assistants. There are also a number of additional support staff, nurses, physiotherapists, speech and language therapists who work in the school. Indeed, the school works in a multi-disciplinary setting, with professionals from Health, Social and Psychological Services and other voluntary bodies.

Blackberry Hill is an attractive one-storey building with an additional autism base. All classrooms are spacious, light and airy, with both carpeted and wet areas. Shared school areas include a sensory room, soft-play room, food technology room, hydrotherapy room, physiotherapy room and small-group teaching and therapy rooms. The school library is situated in a carpeted area adjacent to classrooms and planned to give easy access to all pupils. The hall is large and multi-purpose, serving as a dining hall, school assembly area and gym.

The class

There are eight children in the class. All except one are Reception age. All of the children have Statements, which highlight complex and global learning difficulties. It is a mixed-ability class that is lively and interactive. The classroom is set up as an early years classroom that follows a High Scope theme of 'Plan, do and review', and child-initiated activities. There are activity areas and tables around the classroom that have picture symbols associated with them.

Story time at Blackberry Hill School

The adults

Mrs V., the class teacher, has a BA in Primary Education and MA in Special Education. On leaving college, she worked in a mainstream primary school as a Year 3 teacher. In 1993, she moved to teach in an all-age special school, where she taught mixed ages and abilities in the primary and middle school departments. Mrs V. moved to Blackberry Hill School when it opened in 1998, as an early years co-ordinator and Senior Teacher. She is currently responsible for Reception and Year 1 class. Her curriculum leadership responsibilities include maths, science, language–literacy and inclusion. Mrs V. is a short-term foster parent for a young girl with disabilities.

Miss H., the nursery nurse, qualified with her national nursery nurse qualification in 1990, an additional High Scope course, an advanced diploma in childcare and education and numerous short community education courses. She gained experience as a nanny before doing supply work as a nursery nurse in primary schools in the north east of England. This included six months in a school for children with moderate learning difficulties. Following this, she moved to a school for children with severe and profound learning difficulties where she supported learning across the ages over the three years she was there. Miss H. joined Blackberry Hill when it opened and has supported in several different classes since then.

Mrs M., the class assistant, is a registered child-minder and qualified beauty therapist. She lives in the local area with her family where she was a child-minder for sixteen years. Mrs M. began work at Blackberry Hill school as a mid-day supervisory assistant. She then became a classroom assistant assigned to work on a one-to-one basis with a little girl who has severe epilepsy. Mrs M. is also a classroom assistant in other areas of the school when required.

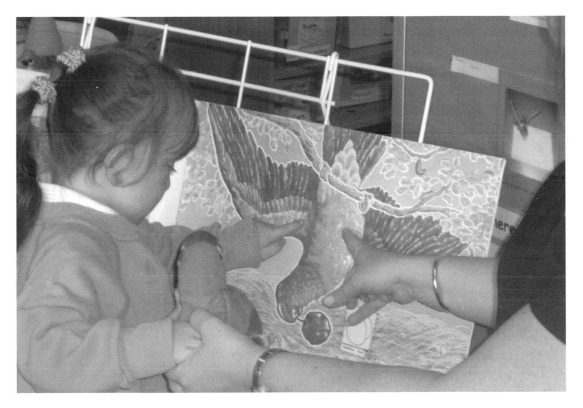

Alison matching objects to the story

The children

Shaun is five years old and has a Statement that specifies severe learning difficulties as a principal focus. English is Shaun's second language at home. His IEP objectives primarily relate to the development of an effective communication system, so that Shaun can make his basic needs known; his self-help skills and also the development of early play and learning skills. Shaun's current targets in the class are:

- *Language and Literacy:* To encourage Shaun to respond to his name through stilling, eye contact and gesture.
- *Maths:* To encourage Shaun to find favourite toys located in familiar places (object permanence).
- *Personal Social Education:* To encourage Shaun to become with familiar with and experience a Doidy cup (a cup designed to move Shaun from a sucking to a drinking action).

Shaun is also following a physiotherapy programme to facilitate his gross and fine motor development.

John is five years old and has Down Syndrome. He has a Statement that specifies severe learning difficulty as a principal focus. John came to Blackberry Hill after attending a community Jewish nursery close to his home. His IEP objectives primarily aim to improve his early expressive and receptive language skills, to further develop his listening skills in a variety of contexts, and to increase his independence skills with particular reference to toileting. John's current targets in class are:

- *Language and Literacy:* To encourage John to recognise and read his own and peers' names in class.
- *Maths:* To encourage John to consolidate his recognition of amounts and match accordingly to three.
- *Personal Social Education:* To encourage John to use the toilet appropriately.

Carol is five years old and her Statement has severe learning difficulties as a principal focus. She also has severe epilepsy, which has to be managed and monitored continuously throughout the school day. Her IEP objectives primarily aim to improve her early expressive and receptive language skills, to encourage her to understand and follow adult requests to comply with familiar classroom routines, and to develop appropriate self-help skills. Carol's current targets in class are:

- *Language and Literacy:* To encourage Carol to spontaneously and functionally use two-word phrases; to encourage Carol to recognise and read the main characters in ORT Stage 1 (Kipper, Mum, Dad, Biff, Chip and Floppy).
- *Maths:* To encourage Carol to count to three and match amounts appropriately; to encourage Carol to consolidate recognition of the numerals to three and to have one-to-one correspondence while counting.
- *Personal Social Education:* To encourage Carol to co-operate with adult-directed tasks for up to fifteen minutes; to encourage Carol to display positive behaviour and co-operate with less familiar members of staff.

Alison is five years old and her Statement has severe learning difficulties as a principal focus. From her IEP, her primary objectives are to improve her communication skills, to improve her fine motor skills, and to increase her independence skills with particular reference to toileting. Alison's current targets in class are:

- *Language and Literacy:* To encourage Alison to spontaneously sign (using Makaton) drink, biscuit, book, dolly, Dad, Mum, sister and teddy.
- *Maths:* To encourage Alison to develop an understanding of one-to-one correspondence.
- *Personal Social Education:* To continue to encourage Alison to use the toilet.

Darren is five years old and his IEP has complex learning disabilities as a principal focus. Darren has learning, physical and medical issues that impact upon his classroom experiences. From his IEP, the primary objectives are to develop his communication skills through speech, signing and gesture, to develop his play and learning skills, to develop his ability to accept direction and his ability to concentrate for longer periods of time. Darren's current class targets are:

- *Language and Literacy:* To encourage Darren to recognise real objects and coloured pictures from a choice of two.
- *Maths:* To encourage Darren to sort and match everyday objects.
- *Personal Social Education:* To encourage Darren to remove his coat and put it back on.

Darren is also following a speech and language programme where his targets are to:

- wave hello;
- develop his use of Makaton signing;
- develop his comprehension of actions through songs;
- introduce him to the Picture Exchange Scheme (PECS).

Mathew is six years old. His Statement has foci of severe learning difficulties, challenging behaviour and speech and language. From his IEP, the primary objectives are to develop Mathew's best possible progress across the curriculum, to encourage the development of expressive communication and to reduce his level of aggressive behaviour to others. His current class targets are:

- *Language and Literacy:* To encourage Mathew to recognise, imitate and use the Makaton signs for Mum, Dad, drink, dinner, stop and goodbye.
- *Maths:* To encourage Mathew to find objects that are in familiar places and put objects back in familiar places (object permanence).
- *Personal Social Education:* To encourage Mathew to understand and respond to 'Stop' with a verbal and signed cue.

Mathew is following a speech and language programme that sets out the importance of using short phrases or sentences when communicating with him, which are supported by signing, gesture, photos and pictures or symbols whenever possible. In general, the programme is directed at increasing the length of time Mathew can be directed in activities, increasing the level of his eye contact and joint attention, and to support his waiting and turn-taking in small groups. His specific communication targets are to:

- develop his understanding in familiar situations, e.g. at snack time, give him a choice of two items and ask him to put the crisp or biscuit on a particular peer's plate (two-word level understanding);
- develop his understanding of actions through songs. Encourage him to imitate actions, then in a group or with toys ask him to do the actions with less prompting;
- develop his understanding of photos or pictures which relate to familiar activities, objects or toys;
- encourage him to look at books. Point things out to him and ask him to 'find . . .';
- continue to encourage him to use his PECS to choose activities;
- encourage him to use the Makaton sign for 'More' within activities;
- encourage him to imitate speech sounds within songs, e.g. animal noises, and when requesting 'More' and 'Please', specifically target the sounds 'M' and 'P'.

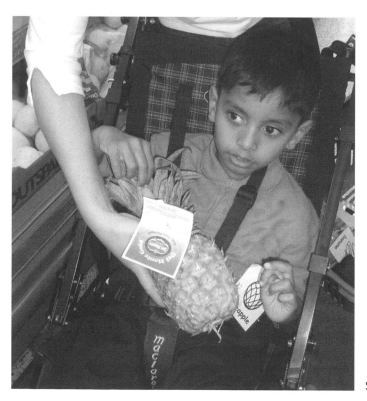

Shopping for items from the story

The lesson

The lesson is a literacy lesson based around the picture book *Honda's Surprise*. The book is used as a focus of a series of lessons in the classroom. The first lesson introduced the book, there was a shared reading, and then the children went shopping for the fruit in the book. The children used picture symbols in the shopping activity. The second lesson shared the story again, this time as a 'story sack' experience, and then the children split into groups for the following activities:

- Fruit exploration and tasting.
- Printing with the fruit.
- Soft dough activity where the children roll and cut animal characters from the book.
- Cooking activity where the children made animal characters from the book.

This best lesson relates to the second lesson.

Shopping with symbols linked to the story

The planning

Long-term planning

See Table 6.1.

Table 6.1 Example of long-term planning at Blackberry Hill School

Topic: Plants/animals	Summer 2003
Curriculum reference	**Objectives**
Knowledge and Understanding of the World, Science, History, Geography, ICT, DT. National Curriculum (NC) REF: Science Sc1 SC2 1ac Sc3 lab ICT la DT la 2a Hist 1a 2a Geog 3abc.	To find out about and identify some living things. To look closely at similarities, differences, patterns and change. To build and construct with a variety of objects. To begin to differentiate between past and present. To operate simple equipment. To discuss and investigate the natural world.
Creative Development Art/ Music. NC REF: Art 1ab 2abc Music 1a 1 b.	To explore colour, texture, shape, form and space in two and three dimensions. To recognise and explore how sounds can be changed, sing simple songs from memory. To recognise repeated sounds and match movements to music. To begin to use imagination in art and design, role-play and stories. To respond in a variety of ways to what they see, hear, smell, touch and feel.
Personal, social and emotional development. PSHE NC Reference: lcde 2acde 3abg.	To maintain attention, concentrate and sit quietly when appropriate. To respond to significant experiences. To form good relationships with peers and adults. To select and use activities and resources independently. To show an awareness of own needs in relation to eating, hygiene and dressing. To understand what is right and wrong, and why.

Medium-term planning

See Table 6.2.

Table 6.2 Example of medium-term planning at Blackberry Hill School

Topic: Plants/animals

Curriculum reference	Focus and objectives	Activities/ strategies	Evaluation/ assessment	Key questions
Knowledge and understanding of the world.	Sand and water: To explore the properties of sand and water.	Playing with animals from story in sand and water.	Record responses and observations in observation booklets and discuss experiences at Smiley Time.	Can the child explore appropriately with the sensory activities?
	Sensory: To respond in a variety of ways to what we hear, smell, touch and feel.	Using cause and effect, light and musical toys.		How does the child respond to tasting fruit?
		Tac Pac session.		How does the child show curiosity?
	Science: To find out about living things and look closely at similarities, differences, patterns and change.	Tasting, exploring, feeling different fruits.		Is the child able to operate the switches – what prompting do they need?
	IT: To operate simple equipment.	Looking at and exploring tadpoles and looking after plants.		Is the child able to show curiosity?
	Construction: To build and construct with a variety of objects.	Using PC with Switch It, Smart Alec, Spot and Jump Ahead – using roller mouse and switch.		
	History and Geography: To discuss and investigate the natural world.			

Short-term planning

Whole class weekly plan

- *Monday:* To listen to familiar nursery rhymes. To encourage children to join in with actions and vocalizations and request nursery rhyme using a symbol or verbal prompt.
- *Tuesday:* To listen to story of *Handa's Surprise*. To be able to find coloured symbols: antelope, monkey, giraffe, zebra, goat, and parrot, and match to the illustration in the book. To encourage children to sign or vocalise the name of animals.
- *Wednesday:* To listen to the book *Handa's Surprise*. To be able to match black and white symbols of fruit to real fruit – passion fruit, mango, tangerine, orange, guava, and avocado pear.
- *Friday:* To be able to listen to story of *Handa's Surprise*. Encourage joining in with the story, signs and refrains. Encourage children to notice when a phrase is missing.

Group tasks or IEP work

(Adults identified to mediate particular activities.)

Monday
- Group 3: to use pens and pencils to develop fine motor control – drawing around jungle animal templates (Mrs V. to lead).
- Group 2: Fine motor – mark-making with animal sponges and paints (Miss H. to lead).
- Group 1: Experiencing and responding one-to-one interactive play routines with animal puppets (Mrs M. to lead).

Tuesday
- Fine motor: Encourage slicing, spreading and cutting with toast at morning break. Encourage choice of spread by verbal, picture or symbol cue. Mathew using PECS system (Mrs V. to lead).
- Groups 2 and 3: Using characters from story with puppets and experience retelling story (Miss H. to lead).

Wednesday
- Group 2: Mark-making with fruit printing (Miss H. to lead).
- Group 1: Sensory experience and tactile exploration of exploring and tasting fruit (Mrs M. to lead).
- Group 3: Fine motor work using cutters and rollers with dough to make animal shapes (Mrs V. to lead).

Friday
- Group 1: Encourage tracking up and down and L–R eye movements with animal puppets (Mrs V. to lead).
- Groups 2 and 3: One-to-one reading – home/school reading books (Miss H. to lead).
- Groups 2 and 3: Listening and responding to animal sounds (Mrs M. to lead).

Tasting the fruit from the story

Plenary/assessment/key questions for the week

Monday
- Discuss group work and review achievement.
- Annotate fine motor work. Can children draw around templates?

Tuesday
- Discuss group work and review achievements.
- Can children slice, spread and cut?

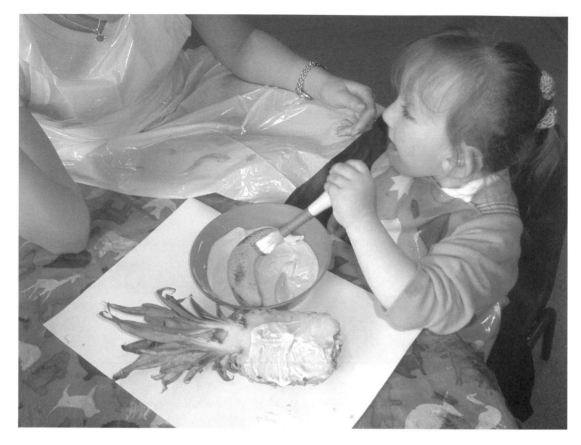

Printing with the fruit from the story

Wednesday
- For Group 1, note reactions to sensory experience.
- For Groups 2 and 3, comment on level of fine motor skills. Hand dominance?

Friday
- Discuss group work and review achievements. Can the children join in with major refrains in story and notice when an animal name is missing?

The lesson began with a repeat of the picture story *Handa's Surprise*, this time as a 'story sack' experience, where there were objects and pictures that the children could handle and explore as the story progressed. The children were then told about the following activity options:

- Fruit exploration and tasting.
- Printing with the fruit.
- Soft dough activity where the children roll and cut animal characters from book.
- Cooking activity where the children make animal character biscuits from the book (this was in the school food technology room).

An adult supported each activity group and the children were able to choose which activity they wanted to do.

Making Play-Dough fruit

Evaluation

All adults in the class felt that the lesson went particularly well. The success of the lesson was explained as all of the children were engaged and on task for sustained periods of time, with the children willingly experimenting and exploring the fruit, particularly the fruit that was unfamiliar to them. There was clear linkage back to the story through the activities. The lesson enabled the adults to focus in on the specific targets for children through the activity, so it provided an appropriate and motivating medium for learning. The adults were able to gather evidence about the children's responses through the key questions they had planned.

CHAPTER 7

Mrs Mopple's Washing Line at Riverview Primary School

Introduction

The school

This is a popular inner-city infant and junior school. The school, which is above average in size, has 383 pupils on roll between the ages of four and eleven years. Most pupils live close to the school and there is a strong demand for places in the SEN classes, which provide specialist provision for pupils with speech and language difficulties, and those with autistic spectrum disorders. Sixty per cent of the pupils are eligible for free school meals, which is well above the national average. Sixty per cent are on the SEN register, which is high, but includes the pupils admitted to the specialist SEN classes. Five per cent of the pupils have a Statement, which is high compared to most schools. Less than three per cent of the pupils are learning English as an additional language. The school admits up to 60 four-year-olds into its Reception classes every year. Initial assessments of the children when entering the school show that their attainment is well below the standards expected of children aged four years. A recent Ofsted report highlights the planning process as being particularly effective in supporting those pupils identified with SEN, including those in the school's speech and language class and the communication class.

The class

The class is an eight-place autistic unit, which is within the mainstream school. The age range within the unit covers the whole of the primary school range. All the children within the unit are diagnosed as having ASD, but they, it has been felt, can cope with inclusion into a mainstream school. Inclusion can be two ways; that is, children from the unit going out into mainstream classes, and sometimes groups of children coming from the mainstream classes into the unit. Children coming into the unit were beneficial for the children who found working in large groups difficult. This allowed them to become

Children from Riverview Primary School in self-directed activities

confident in larger groups, while still maintaining the security of their classroom. It also allowed the children to become familiar with each other in a smaller, more supportive environment. The children in the school saw coming into the class as a privilege and enjoyed working with the pupils with ASD.

The adults

Mrs T. is the class teacher. She is a mum and grandmother, and has 27 years' experience working with children with special educational needs; part of this time has been in mainstream schools. She holds a teaching certificate, a BA Hons (Special Needs), a Certificate in Generic Behaviour in Children and Adolescents, and a Certificate in Autism.

Mrs B. is the teaching assistant. Sign language is her first language: both her parents are profoundly deaf. She is a parent to two teenage boys. She has worked in a private school for the deaf, and has experience working with children with autistic spectrum disorder.

Mrs N. is the one-to-one support for Rowan, who is a pupil in the group. She is also his Nanny. Mrs N. is a qualified nanny and has worked for many years in this field. Her cousin has severe learning difficulties. Rowan's parents pay her to come into school to support him in class. This additional support enables Rowan to stay in class and engage in class activities, with which, staff feel, Rowan would struggle, and even put his placement in mainstream in jeopardy. Rowan and Mrs N. have a very strong, long-term relationship and Mrs N. does not allow him to opt out of what he should be doing. She is able to break down any task he struggles with into very small steps, and gives Rowan lots of praise, which he loves.

The children

Three children out of the group have Statements. They are David, Rowan and Jack. The children in the class are a mixed group of children with ASD and children from the Reception class who were of a similar ability. This was a preparation for two of the children who were going to begin to join the class group for inclusion.

David is six years old and has a full Statement where autistic spectrum disorder is a central focus. David also has moderate learning difficulties. He responds very well to structure and he needs to know what he is going to do. This is done through a visual timetable. David often finds large groups and loud noise very difficult to deal with, and these times prove to be stressful for him. In class, he portrays a strong sense of having to be correct all the time and he becomes quickly distressed if he finds what he is doing is not correct. David's speech is difficult to understand and he appears acutely aware of this, and is often reluctant to speak. He is able to play in parallel with other children and he will watch and copy what they do. However, to be included in their play or other group work, David needs the support of an adult.

Rowan is seven years old and has a Statement where autistic spectrum disorder is a central focus. Rowan also has severe learning difficulties. He has clear speech but also shows a great level of echolalia where he continually repeats things that he has heard which are unrelated to what is going on around him. Rowan can display difficult and challenging behaviour. This is particularly noticeable when he is asked to do something not on his own agenda. He can become defiant and aggressive at these times. Rowan prefers to be by himself and finds interaction and play with any of his class group extremely difficult. In class he displays lots of flapping and repetitive behaviours. In any group context Rowan needs continual one-to-one support. Rowan enjoys stories, particularly story sacks, where he becomes very interested in the objects. He also enjoys joining in familiar and repetitive phrases from the story with an adult. Rowan does not recognise his name when written down, but can spell simple words if spelled using Letter Land, a commercial approach to the teaching of letter names.

Jack is six years old and has a full Statement where autistic spectrum disorder is a central focus. He is a very bright little boy and displays characteristics that form an Asperger type of autism. Jack has huge behaviour issues at home where he is apt to lose his temper, becomes extremely violent and smashes things. In school, he appears very introverted and will cry when asked to do anything. It is suspected that this may be a strategy that allows him not to do what someone else wants him to do. Jack finds play very difficult and stressful. He is reluctant to participate in any social play activity. He needs constant adult support to interact in a play situation. Jack likes to participate in self-chosen activities and will not join in other activities unless drawn in and supported by an adult. Jack has very clear speech. His academic skills of reading, writing and maths are far better than many of his Reception classmates, and are beyond what would be expected for his age. Jack has excellent computer and IT skills, and this is one of his preferred activities.

Children from Riverview Primary School being introduced to the story *Mrs Mopple's Washing Line*

Planning

Long-term planning

Long-term planning for Numeracy and Literacy is in accordance with the strategies (NLS, NNS) for Reception. However, for Reception age children, Foundation stage planning can be used until the term after they are five. Due to the level of deprivation in the school, Foundation Stage planning is often used for longer to ensure that individual learning differences are met. This lesson is placed within the Speaking, Listening and Writing goals of the Early Learning Goals. The overriding theme of the lesson is, 'What do I wear?'

Medium-term planning

See Table 7.1.

Table 7.1 Medium-term planning at Riverview Primary School

Area of learning: ELGs; CLL		
Learning objectives	**Activities**	**Assessment focus**
1. Writes own name with appropriate use of upper and lower case writing.	1. Join in with familiar stories. 2. Copycat games – action songs, stories and rhymes. 3. Identify particular characters. 4. Story sacks. 5. Circle Time games.	
2. Knows that words have meaning.	1. Personal letters in name. 2. Letter hunts in the classroom. 3. Creating letter shapes using dough, collage materials. 4. Computer games. 5. Children are encouraged to write own name on their work.	
	1. Give children the opportunity to add print to the environment. 2. Provide word banks related to topics. 3. Class collections of familiar logos. 4. Instructions written with pictorial support. 5. Shared reading activities.	

Short-term planning

See Table 7.2.

Table 7.2 Short-term planning at Riverview Primary School: *Mrs Mopple's Washing Line*

Area of learning: ELGs; CLL

Learning objectives	Differentiated activities	Adult role/ organisation	Assessment/ evaluation
5e To use talk to take on the role of the character.	Whole group use story sack to re-enact *Mrs Mopple's Washing Line*. Group to take a character out of book. Hang out the washing, each child to take a named article and peg it on the line.	Three adults. TA with Group 1. J to work with RT in Group 3. Class teacher with Group 2.	All group join in and repeat familiar phrases from story. Match words to picture and are able to write own sentence using word bank.
Text level work CLL 6 CLL8 g.			
To think about and discuss what they intend to write ahead of writing it.	**Group 1** To match words to sentences in book. Write their own sentence about the story.		Match pictures. Sequence pictures. Over-write own sentence.
To extend vocabulary especially by grouping and naming.	**Group 2** To match words to pictures using vocabulary from the story. Sequence pictures on work sheet and stick in book. Over-write own sentence.		Match picture to picture. Over-write word from story.
CLL9 Retell narratives in the correct sequence.			
CLL16 Attempt writing for different purposes.	**Group 3** Match picture to picture from the story. Over-write word under picture from the story.		

Individual Education Planning

The targets on the individual IEPs are as follows.

David

Language and Literacy

- David will explore and experiment with words. Criterion for success will be that he will point out words within the texts used. These will be from the Reception Literacy Strategy high frequency word list.
- David will use talk to create imaginary situations. Criterion for success will be that he will act out a familiar story, either in a one-to-one situation or part of a small group.
- David will construct a simple sentence. Criterion will be that he will word match to build sentences.

Mathematics

- David will demonstrate one-to-one correspondence in many everyday situations. Criterion for success will be that he gives out the fruit or biscuits to each child correctly at snack time.
- David will identify smaller and larger quantities visually by comparison. Criterion for success will be that he compares two sets of objects and says which has more and which has less.

Personal Health Social Education

- David will be able to concentrate on a structured activity with little adult support, for five minutes. Criterion for success will be that he will work through the structured task without interruption for the length of the task.

Rowan

Language and Literacy

- Rowan will join in with favourite nursery rhymes, stories and songs. Criterion for success will be that he will sing rhymes and songs and join in familiar phrases in stories.
- Rowan will imitate sounds with his voice. Criterion for success will be that he will sing and say rhymes, after an adult, using different voices modelled.

Mathematics

- Rowan will verbally join in rote counting up to 5. Criterion for success will be that he correctly verbally counts out the number of objects needed for an activity.

- Rowan will recognize numerals 1 to 5. Criterion for success will be that he matches a numeral to a name or quantity of objects.

Personal Health Social Education

Rowan will experience collaboration with others in play. Criterion for success will be that he actively joins in small-group activities and co-operative games.

Jack

Language and Literacy

- Jack will recount simple stories. Criterion for success will be that he successfully retells a variety of narratives using props where appropriate.
- Jack will develop increasing control in his mark-making. Criterion for success will be that he will correctly overwrite words connected to books or themes in the classroom.
- Jack will use talk to take on the role of a character. Criterion for success will be that he successfully re-enacts familiar stories using talk and action.

Looking at clothes from class washing line

Mathematics

- Jack will demonstrate an understanding that when two sets are combined, there will be more than the original set. Criterion for success will be that he successfully physically combines two sets and then verbally explains that there are more.
- Jack will begin to use and understand comparative language. Criterion for success will be that he successfully uses the terms 'big', 'little', 'wide', 'tall', 'light', 'heavy', 'empty', 'full', 'small', 'large' and 'tiny'.

Personal Health Social Education

- Jack will develop confidence to use his peers and adults as partners in his learning. Criterion for success will be that he is able to work in a group of children either in a problem-solving or co-operative activity. An adult will support his interaction with the group.

The lesson

The children listened to the story *Mrs Mopple's Washing Line* read by the teacher, Mrs T.; the children sat around a table. Mrs N. and Mrs B. strategically sat around the table to support child participation in the activity. Once the story was completed, adults and children, led by Mrs T., acted out the story, pretending to wash the clothes (actual clothes) and then taking it in turns to hang them on a line. They then acted out blowing like the wind and the adults blew the washing all over the classroom. The children went off and found pieces of washing. At this point, David, Rowan and Jack had an adult close by who gave verbal and gestural support to them to find a piece of clothing and return to their seats. While the teacher led from the centre of the group, the adults and children around the table together talked about where their pieces of washing were found. The teacher was aware of the other adults' facial and gestural expressions so she could involve David, Rowan and Jack in the whole classroom discussion. The children were redirected to the washing line and a child demonstrated re-hanging the washing. Children in turn hung their item of clothing on the line. A celebration of the complete washing line occurred before the children then went into their small groups. In the small groups children completed their set tasks with adults circulating around the room to support and mediate learning. The lesson ended in the small groups. As the children finished at different times, they progressed on to a different activity.

Hanging out the washing

Evaluation

All adults contributed to the evaluation of the lesson. It was agreed by staff to be highly successful. It was motivating and provided an appropriate medium for the children to work successfully on their IEP targets that are related to Language and Literacy and PSHE. Through the activity, David was able, with adult verbal support, to explore and experiment with words from *Mrs Mopple's Washing Line*. When the washing blew around the classroom, David joined in the blowing and the searching for the clothes. Although there was an adult in close proximity, he did not need direct verbal or gestural support. In the small group setting he independently matched words to build a short sentence. Throughout the initial story-telling David was able to concentrate on the story with minimum gestural support from an adult. He did call out on a number of occasions, but responded well to adult prompting to listen and not talk.

Rowan was able to join in the story, familiar to him, and, with teacher encouragement, joined in familiar phrases of the story. In the small group, Rowan, working directly with Mrs N., imitated two different voices for parts of the story related to the blowing of the washing.

At the beginning of the lesson, in the whole class group context, Jack was able to work in a group of children in this co-operative activity. When the children got up to search for the washing, Jack was offered some verbal adult mediation to build his confidence and support his participation on the noisy and active group activity. During the lesson, Jack demonstrated that he was able to re-enact and recount the story *Mrs Mopple's Washing Line*, using the washing line in the classroom as a prompt. With adult verbal support from Mrs B., Jack was able to imitate the voice of Mrs Mopple. In the small group context he independently overwrote key words from the story. An adult was close by to offer intermittent verbal and gestural support.

On reflection, adults felt that the IEP targets were appropriate for David, Jack and Rowan as they were seen to be within the children's zone of proximal development; that is, not too easy and not too difficult, but at a point where the children could achieve success with some subtle adult mediation. The activity was also seen to be successful in offering an opportunity for the children to work independently and within a group. The former is an area with which this group of children needs a great deal of continuous support. The staff are experienced in working with children with autistic spectrum disorders. Mrs N. has a very strong relationship with Rowan. She knows when to give support and when to let him work independently. She is able to moderate the group where he is working, so that everyone has a turn and there is not domination from the most able children. The use of appropriate verbal support and praise by all adults helped the children feel good about their participation and contributed to their motivation in the activity.

CHAPTER 8

Reflections: the importance of positive attitudes, procedures and strategies

INTRODUCTION

This chapter reflects on each of the four stories of the teachers' best inclusive lessons. The reflection of these stories demonstrates that the development of greater inclusive practice for a diverse range of learners is clearly related to teacher attitudes, classroom procedures, and teaching and learning strategies. From these we can begin to elicit views, processes, procedures and strategies that seem to be particularly pertinent for promoting effective inclusive teaching in other early years settings. We will also consider each teacher's interpretation of inclusion, as reflected in the choice of their 'best inclusive lesson'. The classroom practices embedded in this book will be synthesised and presented as potentially helpful to teachers and practitioners who are eager to promote greater inclusive practice in other early years settings. A model of pupil learning is discussed that integrates a process for learning. In the conclusion, this model of learning is then applied to the adults' professional development. This is because there is one certainty in inclusive practice – that things change. It is the adult's ability to change and participate in continued professional improvement that can also be seen to be instrumental for developing greater inclusive practice.

Reflections on the best lessons

'Jungle Journeys' at Summerfield Glade School

The adults involved in the lesson collectively reflected on how the lesson had gone. They felt that during the whole class activity there was excellent attention given to story by all the children in the group. The activity afforded a medium where all of the children worked within their IEP targets, not only with success, but also in a fun and motivating way. It appears for this 'best lesson', that effective inclusion is being interpreted as a shared group experience with the opportunity for children also to work on activities that are tailored to their individual needs. The teacher appears to be interpreting inclusion as a joint, but different, experience where individual learning needs drive the teaching and learning, but the dynamic of the whole class offers an important shared experience where children are introduced to new learning and practice, and also celebrate that new learning.

The story itself was a familiar one to the children. Working with the familiar, and giving an additional 'twist' or tangent, is a successful approach to motivating and involving children in their learning. Children are given a concrete opportunity where they are able to bring previous knowledge to the experience. It allows children to begin their learning at a place where they feel comfortable and safe, and allows them to take risks in their learning in a supported and familiar context. Sometimes the newness of an activity can be exciting and a great motivator. However, the learning experience is different and the child may need support to engage in the new and different learning, rather than support to apply previous knowledge to a new situation. In this example the twists that were added to the story experience were highly practical and engaging, and allowed the children to engage actively with most of their senses (hearing, touching and seeing). In this way the story became alive for them, and indeed allowed high levels of participation on their part.

The children feel comfortable with the central focus of the lesson to be able to take risks in their learning and engage with individually challenging learning experiences. This was exemplified in this best lesson account with the animal hunts. An animal hunt had been successfully carried out in class with the children, and this was then extended to the wider context of the school.

The individual needs in this class at Summerfield Glade are broad, varied and highly complex. The planning of the lesson was detailed, and clearly set out how the individual learning of children was being integrated into the wider curriculum demands. The nature of the individual learning needs was both academic and social, highlighting the importance of ensuring that planning reflects this holistic perspective of development. In the short-term planning of the lesson, the teacher adopted the 'all, most and few' structure of setting out learning targets of the curriculum. This approach is becoming more widely used since the QCA project on curriculum guidelines for pupils with learning difficulties (QCA, 2001) highlighted it as potential good practice. This structure allows some manageability between the often daunting curriculum demands and the group learning needs of a particular class. At Summerfield Glade we see the structure used effectively to focus upon writing and reading targets. The progression of the lesson over the week is an excellent example of how the focus of a lesson is more than a 60-minute session. The cumulative effect of the learning allows the management of graduated learning experiences across a longer time period. This is something that is also shown at Blackberry Hill and offers opportunities to the children to return to new learning and apply and reapply it in different ways. The structure of the lesson, with a beginning group sharing, individual and small groups and then a plenary, shows the effectiveness of peer and individual learning where the interaction between the learners forms an integral part of the learning process.

'Musical Melodies' at Springfield First School

This lesson illustrates an example of how inclusion is being perceived in relation to a little boy with challenging behaviour. For the adults at Springfield, this best lesson in inclusion involved this little boy conforming and meeting the same expectation as the other children in the group. Having a child (or children) with challenging behaviour in the classroom is a well-known source of adult stress, and is highlighted as an often insurmountable challenge for inclusion. Extremely challenging behaviour by one child (or a group of children) can indeed influence the atmosphere of a class in a negative way. A natural worry about this is that the other children in the class have a negative and stressful experience. However, when the adults have the strategies and procedures to support children with challenging behaviour, the intensity of the impact is greatly reduced. When the disruption is managed to a minimum, all children experience this effective management and the outbursts have less impact. We see this at Springfield First School with one little boy. At this point, the adults were able to support Peter in a structured way in the natural context of the classroom. However, there may become a point with Peter, or other children who have similar challenging behaviour, when additional adult assistance is required. It is important that Peter is able to receive appropriate support for his individual needs, but it is also important that this happens in a way that does not take away from the needs of the whole class. Sometimes we hear of examples when this balance does not occur, often in the name of inclusion, but to the detriment of learning for all children.

Mrs H. and Mrs S. both participated in the reflection of the lesson. They felt the activity was clearly highly motivating for all the children. It was a familiar, safe, but exciting activity in which the children wanted to participate. Peter was keen to participate and chose, himself, to return to the activity and behave appropriately. Peter did have a challenging outburst when he became frustrated at having to wait his turn. Mrs H. responded to him in a calm, consistent and firm manner. She adopted a classroom procedure that was well established in the class: inviting him back in, but reiterating the classroom expectations. Mrs H. had her expectations for the group and made it clear to Peter that he, too, had to meet those to be part of the activity. She did, however, offer him support strategies to rejoin the group. These included physical proximity to her, and also praise for appropriate behaviour.

Parts of this lesson for Peter and Mrs H. were highly stressful. We hear about the early experiences that Peter has had and how these can help to explain his current, impulsive behaviour. However, the expectations of the classroom remained constant and, although they were difficult for Peter, he was supported with familiar procedure to respond positively to them. The well-established classroom procedures helped enormously to bring about the teacher's desired outcome. Indeed, after a short time away from the group, Peter chose to rejoin, sitting close to the teacher for support, and successfully completed the activity.

When children display challenging behaviour it can be a natural response for the adult to take control of the situation and manage the situation for the child. This is a well-used and effective strategy for children who need support to maintain control of their behaviour. This is an example of external control (that of the adults) managing behaviour. However, it is essential that the focus of control of behaviour moves away from the adult to the child. We do not want a society of children becoming adults who need to have external controls of their behaviour all the time! This illustrates the need to nurture internal control by the child of their own behaviour. This is effectively done by setting up a situation where the child has a choice about his or her behaviour and the adult is there to explain the choices and potential consequences of such choices. In this example, when Peter angrily left the group, Mrs H. in a supportive and firm way set out the choices for Peter, and asked him to choose. It took him a while, but he did choose to rejoin, probably because the desire to play the triangle was so strong that he was able to accept the taking turns.

The planning of the lesson, in Summerfield Glade School, reflects how individual needs and curriculum demands can be integrated to allow opportunities for children to engage appropriately with curricular, while focusing upon individual, targets. For Peter, this was an extremely valuable learning opportunity about taking turns and sharing power, something he must develop in order to progress through the school successfully. For the other children, this was a valuable musical activity where they, too, had to wait their turn.

What we see at Springfield First School is the power of well-established procedures and routines that are explicit to adults and children. This leads to a level of confidence by the adults, which helps to diffuse stress. The outburst did not adversely impact on the activity; staff reflected that the aims for the activity were successfully met for all children. The procedures set up in the classroom allowed Mrs H. to deal with Peter while Mrs S. continued calmly with the planned lesson.

'Fantastic Fruit' at Blackberry Hill School

At Blackberry Hill School, it appears, for this 'best lesson', that effective inclusion is being interpreted as individualised teaching and learning in a whole class context. At the school we meet a group of children with learning needs that are severe, complex and diverse. The class shares a joint experience, but individual learning is mediated at all times by the adults in the classroom. When reflecting on why the lesson was so successful for this group of learners at this time, there are particular points that can be discussed that demonstrate good practice.

Clearly, the central focus of the book worked well in this classroom of young children with a wide range of severe and complex learning difficulties. Both adults and children enjoyed the story, and the story opened up a variety of activities that supported appropriate child involvement and engagement. The nature of the book (an African story) allowed the lesson to have elements that would also bridge the different cultural backgrounds of the children. It was known that Shaun has previously had experience of pineapples and mangoes at home, and this provided a great point to share with all of the children. The knowledge of the adults in relation to the children was indeed a helpful factor in the effectiveness of the lesson. The high level of understanding allowed the adults to mediate individual learning within the group activity. This met individual learning needs and supported the feeling that the activities were personally meaningful. The activities were planned in an open format, but the mediation was a very carefully structured process. In order to do this, adults in a classroom need to know and understand the individual learning needs of pupils, wider curriculum demands, and appropriate teaching and learning strategies. This takes time, development and energy among the staff team. However, this knowledge allows all adults the understanding and skills to mediate and scaffold learning at the point of the child's entry into the learning activity. This will vary between children, but also vary with the same child across time, depending on other factors – for example, medical, emotional or physiological factors. The way the adults work together as a team in this classroom definitely contributes to the success of the lesson.

In a reflective discussion, the adults at Blackberry Hill talked about how they knew each other's strengths and jointly planned their participation in the lessons around these strengths. They are also constantly aware of what is happening in other parts of the classroom so that they can offer quiet support when needed. In this example, the collaborative practices in the classroom appear clear and the roles and responsibilities of each adult are shared. Although the teacher does the main bulk of the planning, other adults contribute their opinions and advice. The practical teaching in the class is shared, with all adults having an opportunity to lead particular activities if they wish to. This is referred to as co-teaching within the group, where the teacher has ultimate responsibility for the quality of teaching and learning. When one adult is leading, the others are in the class group supporting the engagement of the children.

All adults participate in the collaborative process of record-keeping that the teacher ultimately manages. The adults here expressed their feelings of confidence and the fact that they felt well supported working with the children. They also know the strengths of the children, as well as the areas of focus for development, and are eager to use these strengths in the activities. The nature of the lesson allowed a shared community focus in the classroom that was motivating and engaging for the children, and also supported shared peer experience and interaction. The activities developed supported a multiple intelligence approach to teaching and learning.

Mrs Mopple's Washing Line at Riverview Primary School

It appears for this 'best lesson', that effective inclusion is being interpreted as when a lesson is able to offer the whole group of children a shared activity that meets different needs within the group. The group of children at Riverview Primary School demonstrated a diverse range of learning needs, but a shared emphasis was on the development of social communication. All adults contributed to the evaluation of the lesson and it was agreed by staff to be a highly successful lesson for the whole group of children. This is an example of a lesson that is a stand-alone event which happens at one point in the school day. It is a new activity that the adults introduced to the children and then mediated their participation. The staff in the classroom felt that the central focus upon the story was motivating, and provided an appropriate medium, similar to all of the other examples we have heard about, for the children to work successfully on their IEP targets. The story of *Mrs Mopple's Washing Line* and subsequent activities allowed children short, but structured, opportunities to be part of larger and smaller learning groups. The practical involvement offered the children a point of access into the activity that they could do individually, but share collectively.

One comment by the adults in their reflection was the detail and appropriate level of the children's IEP targets. Children worked successfully to them in their individual work. The targets themselves were seen by staff to be within each child's zone of proximal development. This clear targeting on individual objectives in a larger group setting enabled staff to feel confident about supporting effective and appropriate learning. When staff are confident in the learning experience, so are children. When staff begin to be hesitant, so do children. This level of confidence also has something to do with staff experience. In this example, Mrs N. is very experienced with Ryan: they know each other extremely well. She knows when to give support and when to let him work independently. She was also able to moderate the group sensitively so that the child with the most ability did not dominate the group. This enabled Ryan and other learners to have a turn and experience success. Staff in the room felt that the use of appropriate verbal support and praise by all adults helped all of the children feel good about their participation, and contributed to their motivation in the activity.

Another element of this lesson is the system in which it took place. The school is a school that is committed to developing greater inclusive practice. The staff in the classroom felt that this created an atmosphere of acceptance and celebration in every classroom and across the school as a whole. The children in the school had grown in the inclusive atmosphere, never seeing any child as different but as individuals. Indeed, the staff commented that they had only ever experienced problems between children when children joined school at a later date. This supports the importance and strength of developing inclusive practice from a systems perspective.

Reflections on inclusion from the teachers' perspectives

Reflecting upon the teachers' interpretations of inclusion by their choice and discussions of their best inclusive lessons illustrates the similar and different ways inclusion is being translated into classroom practice. The strong similarity that has come through all of the accounts is the need for a lesson not only to meet the group needs of the class, but also the individual needs of the children. In each of the accounts, attention has been paid to having a shared class activity that in some way also meets the individual learning needs of the children. This is an example of differentiation in practice and strengthens the argument that, for successful inclusion to take place, teachers must be skilled in the strategies and procedures of differentiation.

We saw the interpretation of the individualization being different but equally effective between Summerfield Glade and Blackberry Hill Schools. At Summerfield Glade the children were assigned particular activities that met individual needs, and at Blackberry Hill the child chose the activity but the adult mediated the participation to meet individual needs. This tells us that, indeed, inclusion is not a one-formula solution that applies across all groups of children, but that it is a responsive process that reflects the strengths of the adults and the children in the class. However, essential fundamental attitudes, procedures and strategies are the foundation of an effective responsive process. We will now discuss these in more detail.

Attitudes

In a classroom that supports greater inclusive practice, the teacher's attitudes towards 'difference' are essential. Such differences relate to the learning needs of the children in their class and to their role as teachers. The adults in these accounts demonstrate a positive attitude towards all of the children in their classes. They see all of the children in their classes – whatever their ability and learning differences – as learners. They understand learning differences and are willing to be flexible and adapt to individual needs. This requires a readiness to work collaboratively with other professionals, parents and staff to meet the diverse needs in their classroom. The role of the teacher changes in a collaborative context: she becomes the manager of a team of people. She must be willing to listen actively to the perspectives of others and integrate such perspectives into classroom practice. Collaborative working involves skills that are not necessarily taught in training programmes. Examples of the range of skills involved in collaborative practice are: systems management and people management, including managing meetings, active listening, conciliation, managing paperwork, and translating issues into practice. For some teachers, these skills come naturally, but for others they must be explicitly developed and practised. A willingness to want to develop them is essential in the development of greater inclusive classroom practice. Collaboration will be highlighted again later as an effective strategy for teaching and learning in an inclusive classroom.

We saw at Riverview Primary School that it is important also to foster positive attitudes between children. The systemic attitude of the school was seen by adults in the classroom to have a strong influence on the ambience and attitude of all of the children. The problems in attitude they encountered were with children new to the school who had not yet been influenced by the positive systemic attitudes to diversity.

Procedures

The procedures that are set up in a classroom are fundamental to the success of meeting diverse needs in the classrooms. Procedures help children and adults to know what the expectations of the classroom are, and, equally important, what the implications are for meeting and not meeting these expectations. Sometimes children are expected to know these procedures telepathically without being taught them. It is assumed that, because they enter the classroom, they know the procedures particular to that setting. This is a misguided assumption on the part of adults and can lead to difficult behaviour in the classroom. Procedures have to be taught and practised (and continually practised) by children and adults. Procedures can relate to behaviour and discipline as well as teaching and learning structures. Procedures are embedded in classroom expectations and routines. Procedures are the infrastructure of the classroom: the implicit bricks and mortar that make the classroom strong. When there are issues with behaviour across a group of children, strengthening and clarifying procedures is indeed a helpful first point of reflection and action. Procedures can relate to whole class groups, small peer collaborative groups, and individual children. Indeed, procedures in the classroom can follow a similar staging that we were introduced to in Summerfield Glade School in relation to planning: procedures that relate to all children in the class, procedures that relate to most children in the class, and procedures that relate to a few children in the class.

Examples of procedures that support teaching and learning that have emerged through the accounts of best lessons relate to structures of total communication, models of collaborative practice and planning. At Blackberry Hill School, a system of total communication using signing, symbols and talking, positively supported the involvement of children in meaningful and challenging activities. In the past, this particular approach to teaching and learning remained in the domain of the special school, where, it was considered, only children who have difficulty with learning need to have symbols to support their learning. However, this situation is changing, and in many early years contexts, we see the effective employment of symbols to help scaffold children's learning.

In all of the accounts, we have been given insights into collaborative models of working. This collaboration has been particularly strong between adults and between children as in Blackberry Hill School and Summerfield Glade. Collaborative practice is a highly recommended strategy for developing greater inclusive practice. Collaborative practice sometimes needs to be nurtured in a team. To promote effective collaborative practice, the teacher, as manager of the process, must support the development of:

- clear guidelines of different roles and responsibilities in the classroom;
- a system that allows all adults to express their views and contribute to planning and evaluation;
- a system that supports continued professional development of all adults;
- effective conflict management strategies within the group of adults.

At Springfield First School, the collaboration presented in the planning showed the consultation model. It showed how other adults from the school and county are involved in the planning of some of the learning. Some participate in teaching, but some offer consultations to the teacher. At Summerfield Glade School we see examples of peer collaboration where children are grouped to support each other, exemplified in this picture of two children completing their crocodile pictures together.

Children at Summerfield Glade School working together on individual crocodile pictures

The planning across all of the accounts of the best inclusive lessons share detail and the ability of the teachers to link curriculum demands with individual learning needs. This process allows the identification of particular activities, and teaching and learning strategies before the lesson. Detailed planning is a cornerstone of effective teaching and learning in a classroom with a wide range of learners. However, we have found from the examples here that detailed planning does not have to stifle learning, but enables the adults the knowledge and understanding to scaffold individual and group learning. We see this with Mrs N. at Riverview Primary School with Ryan and the class group, Miss H. with Shaun at Blackberry Hill School, Mrs S. and Laura at Summerfield Glade School and, of course, Mrs H. and Peter at Springfield First School.

Strategies for teaching and learning

A fundamental model of teaching and learning that promotes the inclusion of diverse learners must be explicit. This model includes the following steps:

- Explain
- Model
- Rehearse
- Reinforce
- Practise
- Reflect

Explain

This is where the teacher explains and sets up the learning. In the stories in this book, these have been at the whole class group level. The teacher explains to the children what they are going to do, and expectations are made about what the children will do. It will be necessary, as in the 'Musical Melodies' account, to repeat these expectations at the individual level. It is at the 'Explain' step that the children are first encouraged to join the learning and we see, through the accounts presented here, that the teachers have chosen activities that are motivating for all of the children in the class. It is interesting that three out of the four accounts chose a picture book as the central focus of the lesson. Picture books are a wonderful medium for learning. They not only provide a shared point of focus, a familiar and therefore safe structure for learning, but also are beautifully malleable. You can indeed do almost anything with a picture book: Mathematics, Language and Literacy, Creative, Knowledge and Understanding of the World and IEP targets. All of the books in these accounts relate primarily to Language and Literacy targets, but were also shown to apply to other curriculum areas. In 'Jungle Journeys', 'Fantastic Fruit' and *Mrs Mopple's Washing Line*, the picture books were applied in a way that spanned all of the ability levels of the children in the classes, as well as providing a point of shared interest. In 'Fantastic Fruit' we were given an example of a story that also bridged the cultural diversity of the classroom.

Model

This is where the teacher models the learning. Modelling of desired learning behaviour can occur at the group and individual level. However, with more diverse learners in the classroom, the modelling may need to be repeated and repeated at the individual level. Modelling is a process that shows the learners what they need to do in order to reach the goals set by the teacher. In order for modelling to be successful, it must be very explicit and clear. Modelling can be verbal, as in the 'Musical Melodies' story, where the teacher talks Peter through the process of the learning he is about to engage with: 'You need to wait your turn, and then you will have a go on the triangle'. Or in *Mrs Mopple's Washing Line*, where children are told what to do with the items of clothing. Modelling can also be physical, as in the 'Fantastic Fruit' and 'Jungle Journeys' lessons, where the children are given a physical model to copy. It is important to remember that through modelling we teach desired behaviours that are adult initiated. It is also important to encourage child-initiated exploration in learning that may have little to do with teacher objectives but a lot to do with individual child exploration and expression. A balance between the two is preferred at the early years stage of learning. For example, this balance is demonstrated in 'Fantastic Fruit' where the learning activities of shopping, printing, tasting, physical investigation and modelling were chosen to allow teacher-directed and child-initiated learning to occur.

Rehearse

This is where the child rehearses the learning with the teacher. This step of rehearsal is essential in demonstrating to the child the desired learning. An example of this is in the 'Jungle Journeys' account where the children rehearse with the adult spelling out the word 'snake' with magnetic letters. The rehearsal between adult and child not only allows the child to experience physically, with support, a successful behaviour, but also demonstrates to the adult that the child has the desired behaviour in his or her repertoire. For children who experience difficulties with their learning, this stage of joint rehearsal may need to be repeated many times and also returned to if the learner shows subsequent confusion. We saw in 'Musical Melodies' that Peter and Mrs H. are very much in this stage of rehearsal of turn-taking. Throughout the teachers' accounts, we see examples of strategies employed by adults to support the rehearsal of the desired learning. These strategies included:

- Visual cueing
- Physical and gestural cueing
- Verbal mediation

An example of visual cueing is given in *Mrs Mopple's Washing Line* where the teacher has a washing line set up with pegs in the classroom. An adult places the first item of clothing on the line. The children in the class now have a visual cue to refer to when it is their turn to place their clothing on the washing line. In 'Fantastic Fruit' we see the visual cueing done through the use of picture symbols. When the children are out in the community shopping for the fruit from the book, they refer to their symbol card.

Child at Blackberry Hill School using a symbol of fruit

Visual cueing is a powerful strategy in learning that offers a focus of support for learning. Physical and gestural support also offers effective strategies for rehearsing desired learning. This is where the teacher physically guides the learner in the learning activity. This can be as obvious as hand-over-hand support, or as subtle as an eye-pointing gesture between adult and child. In 'Fantastic Fruit' we see an example of the adult physically prompting Shaun to explore the pineapple.

In 'Jungle Journeys' we see an example of gestural cueing between adult and child in the individual worksheet activity. The teacher is mediating the learning through her employment of gestural (and verbal) cueing.

Verbal mediation occurs naturally throughout most of our teaching; the gentle and continuous verbal support we give to reinforce desired behaviour is an effective teaching strategy for whole class work. Verbal mediation is also effective at an individual level, as demonstrated in 'Musical Melodies'. Mrs H. engaged in verbal mediation to support and rehearse Peter's desired behaviour and returned to it when his behaviour deteriorated. During the period of stress for Peter, Mrs H. was able to return to familiar verbal mediation processes to support Peter's re-entry into the group. At this point she did not introduce anything new into the mediation, but simply and clearly reiterated a statement previously established.

Using objects as part of the story experience

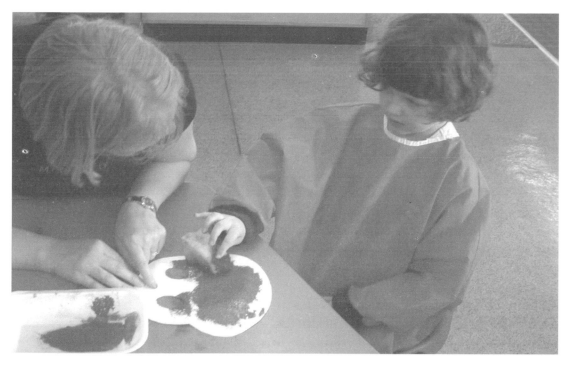

Adult at Summerfield Glade School employing gestural and verbal prompting strategies

Reinforce

This is where the teacher reinforces the expected behaviour in the learning activity. Reinforcement is the cornerstone of learning theory and is where behaviour is established through the support of desired events. Basically, for behaviour to become established, learning theory suggests that it must be reinforced. This reinforcement can be extrinsic or intrinsic. Extrinsic reinforcement refers to events directed towards the learner from outside. This can be from an adult or a peer. Intrinsic reinforcement refers to events or feelings that come from within the person that provide a strengthening of the desired behaviour. We see an example of extrinsic reinforcement in *Mrs Mopple's Washing Line* where an adult verbally supports David while he is part of a larger group. This verbal support came from an adult with whom David has an established relationship. Her close presence behind David also helped to reinforce his physical presence in the larger group of children. An example of intrinsic reinforcement comes in 'Jungle Journeys', where the children are so motivated to join in the school animal hunt that they eagerly participate in the desired learning of identifying animal puppets from symbols. We can reinforce in a physical or verbal way. The way we reinforce desired behaviours in learning is crucial. Initially, reinforcement needs to be constant and repeated in order to establish behaviours. However, the reinforcement must link directly to the behaviour for it to be meaningful. This suggests that reinforcement must be specific and targeted. In the examples of the teachers' accounts, the individual targets, for some children from their IEP, provide the foci of the reinforcement in the learning.

Practice

This is where the learner gets to practise his or her new learning. A well-respected American teacher educator, Fred Jones, suggests that practice is an essential part of learning that we often rush through to the detriment of the establishment of preferred behaviours (Jones, 2003). When new learning is practised, it is the time where such learning is applied to different contexts: where the learner generalises his or her learning. New learning in the classroom often occurs in very structured and orchestrated scenarios. For many learners, when these structures change, difficulties occur. It is important to offer children systematic and supported opportunities to practise their learning. The 'Fantastic Fruit' account demonstrates this with the shopping expedition, and the story of 'Jungle Journeys' shows the important role of the plenary in allowing children an opportunity to practise their learning.

Reflect

This is where the learners get an opportunity to reflect on their learning successes and consider, in an appropriate and supportive way, the application of that learning. We have seen it here in the examples of lessons that have a plenary, in particular at Summerfield Glade School. A reflection of learning soon after the learning has occurred will help the child to revisit the successful learning and give another opportunity for reinforcement.

Conclusion

These stories of teachers' best lessons have afforded a detailed insight into how inclusion is being perceived and practised in four classroom settings. There are differences in the accounts that represent the importance of context, flexibility and working to adult (and children's) interests and strengths. This tells us that there is no one formula for developing greater inclusive practice. Such developments occur within a system that is influenced by wider national attitudes, initiatives and policies, more local school attitudes, initiatives and policies and the immediate context of the classroom. We see at Riverview Primary how the positive systemic direction of the school towards including children with diverse learning needs positively impacted upon the community of the school as a whole. There are also similarities that have been demonstrated to run across these four accounts that represent helpful approaches, procedures and strategies that have been shown to be effective in the context of these best lesson accounts. The model for teaching and learning that has been discussed here relates to the children as learners. However, it is also important to consider the model in relation to the continued professional development of adults within the inclusive classroom. The model is equally applicable to adults. Adults in the classroom:

- need to have new knowledge and strategies explained to them (Explain);
- will benefit from actually seeing particular strategies models, be they mediating, scaffolding, etc.; they need to have an opportunity to rehearse, preferably before they work with children (Model);
- need to have receive feedback and reinforcement about their own new learning (Reinforce);
- need to have opportunities to practise, practise and practise too! It takes an adult, on average, nine full weeks to learn something new and have the new learning assimilated into the human brain – so this practice is an essential component of that (Practice);
- need to participate in focused critical reflection of practice so that the emphasis is on continual improvement and development rather than making do with what is there (Reflect).

In the introduction to this chapter it was suggested that the professional development of the adults in the inclusive classroom is a major influencing factor on the effectiveness of such provision. In the accounts of best lessons presented, greater inclusive practice is achievable even though it is a detailed, complex and often subtle process. In order to rise to the challenge of developing greater inclusive practice, we need to meet the professional training needs of all of the adults who work with the children, not just in the class but also in the school context. In this, training issues of attitude, belief, school and classroom procedures, as well as teaching and learning strategies, must form a central focus.

Glossary

Autistic Spectrum Disorder (ASD)

Children with autistic spectrum disorders have issues with social communication. This group of children, in the past, would have been referred to as autistic. However, because children's abilities and intensities of social communication issues can vary tremendously, the idea of a continuum or spectrum has become more widely accepted to reflect the differences. Further information about ASD can be found at www.nas.co.uk.

Asperger Syndrome

This refers to children with ASD who are very high achievers/gifted in one or more academic areas of the curriculum. This group of children requires appropriate support for their social communication issues and also for their talents. Again, further information about Asperger Syndrome can be found at www.nas.co.uk.

Doidy cup

This is part of a range of aids to eating, such as plates, cups, spoons and non-slip mats that are designed to help children to manipulate utensils more easily when they are learning independence skills. A Doidy cup is designed for easy handling and is non-spill, for children who are learning independence skills.

Individual Education Plan (IEP)

The Individual Education Plan is a learning plan designed to meet individual learning needs on a short- and medium-term basis. Teachers, with the support of SENCOs and others, design the plan. In practice, the IEP is reviewed termly.

Letterland

A commercial program designed to teach letter names, shapes and sounds. Each letter has a character that the child is introduced to through stories, songs and activities. The character is linked to the letter, e.g. King is the letter K.

Makaton

A system of communication that integrates gesture and verbal communication. Makaton was designed for people with learning difficulty as a strategy to support the development of verbal communication. Community Speech and Language Therapists will have information about local courses in your area. Makaton symbols are also used to depict the gestural signs. These symbols are used to support literacy activities as well as visual scheduling.

Mannoy utensils

This is a range of aids to eating, such as plates, cups, spoons, non-slip mats, that is designed to help children to manipulate utensils more easily when they are learning independence skills.

Multiple Intelligences

Multiple intelligence is a theory of intelligence that acknowledges the various forms of intelligence a person has. Gardner (1991) is the grandfather of multiple intelligence theory, which has been developed and applied to learning theory. Gardner has proposed seven (possibly eight) intelligences that differ from one another. These are: linguistic, spatial, logical-mathematical, bodily kinesthetic, music, interpersonal, intrapersonal and naturalist. There are many books currently available concerning multiple intelligences in the classroom. Further information on multiple intelligences can be found on: www.thomasarmstrong.com/multiple_intelligences.htm.

National Literacy Strategy (NLS)

This is the strategy set by the government that all schools must follow for Literacy. There are QCA and NLS guidelines for pupils with learning difficulty. The DfES website (www.dfes.gov.uk) and NLS website (www.nls.gov.uk) can take you to these guidelines.

National Numeracy Strategy (NNS)

This is the strategy set by the government that all schools must follow for Numeracy. There are QCA and NNS guidelines for pupils with learning difficulty. The DfES website (www.dfes.gov.uk) and NNS website (www.nns.gov.uk) can take you to these guidelines.

Oro motor

This is the movement of the mouth, and oro motor activities are designed to support the development of mouth movements.

Picture Exchange Scheme (PECS)

A highly structured and developmental approach using pictures and symbols that supports the development of child-initiated communication. It was initially developed for children with autistic spectrum disorder. A symbolic representation is used to teach the child to 'request' something. Initially, this is very adult supported, but as the child moves through the programme, the adult support is reduced and the nature of the 'requests' becomes more complex. The National Autistic Society has information on courses for PECS.

Special Educational Needs Co-ordinator (SENCO)

Each school and early years provision must have (or have access to) a special educational needs co-ordinator. This co-ordinator attends additional training to support children with learning difficulties. The support that is offered by the co-ordinator can be direct (working with children in class or the school) or indirect (working with staff on a consultative basis outside the classroom).

Statement of Special Education

This is a legal document drawn up by the Local Education Authority that sets out a child's individual learning needs and the provision that is needed to meet those needs. In principle it is developed through a multi-professional assessment that includes professionals, parents and, where appropriate, the child. The Statement of Special Education is formally reviewed annually.

Story sacks

Story sacks is an approach to sharing stories that is intended to make the experience more engaging, motivating and meaningful. Objects (or symbols) from the story are used to support the telling and retelling of the story. These objects tend to be collected in a sack; hence the term, story sacks.

Visual schedule

Visual schedules are an integral part of many approaches to teaching and learning. In a visual schedule, children use pictures, symbols or objects of reference to sequence their day. It is likened to a concrete timetable. Children have to be taught how to manage the schedule, but once this is established, they can be involved in deciding their daily events and activities. Makaton symbols tend to be widely used in visual scheduling. An object of reference is an object (or part of an object) that is used to represent an activity or event, for example, a particular cup is used to represent drink, a particular towel is used to represent swimming, etc.

Zone of Proximal Development

The Zone of Proximal Development was introduced in the work of Vygotsky (1978) and suggests that rather than having a level of development that is lateral, children have a zone that is horizontal as well as lateral. More experienced people (children and adults) help a child move through the Zone of Proximal Development to higher levels through careful mediation and scaffolding of learning. Mediation and scaffolding refers to the support strategies and procedures that are conducive to learning.

References

Acheson, D. (1998) *Independent Inquiry into Inequalities in Health Reports.* London: The Stationery Office.

Aird, R. (2001) *The Education and Care of Children with Severe, Profound and Multiple Learning Difficulties.* London: David Fulton.

Alexander, R. (2000) *Culture and Pedagogy: International Comparisons in Primary Education.* Oxford: Blackwell.

Baglin, C. and Bender, M. (1994) *Handbook on Quality Childcare for Young Children: Setting Standards and Resources.* California: Singular Press.

Barnes, C. (1996) 'Theories of Disability and the Origins of Oppression of Disabled People in Western Society', in Barton, L. (ed.) *Disability and Society: Emerging Issues and Insights.* Harlow: Longman.

Berger, A., Morris, D. and Portman, J. (2000) *Implementing the National Numeracy Strategy for Pupils with Learning Difficulties.* London: David Fulton.

Bruce, T., Whalley, M., Mairs, K., Arnold, C. and the Centre team (2001) 'Case Study Two: A Family Centre', in Pascal, C. and Bertram, T. (2001) *Effective Early Learning: Case Studies in Improvement.* London: Paul Chapman.

Carpenter, B. (1998) *Families in Context.* London: David Fulton.

Carpenter, B., Ashdown, R. and Bovair, K. (1996) *Enabling Access.* London: David Fulton.

Carpenter, B., Ashdown, R. and Bovair, K. (2001) *Enabling Access* (2nd edition). London: David Fulton.

Clarke, K. and Jones, P. (2000) 'Parental Perspectives', in Moore, M. (2000) *Insider Perspectives on Inclusion.* Sheffield: Philip Armstrong Publications.

Contact a Family (www.cafamily.org.uk).

Cook, T. and Swain, J. (2001) 'In the Name of Inclusion: "We all, at the end of the day, have the needs of the children at heart"', *Critical Social Policy: A Journal of Theory and Practice in Social Welfare*, Vol. 21, No. 2, May.

Corbett, J. (2001) 'Teaching Approaches which Support Inclusive Education: A Connective Pedagogy', *British Journal of Special Education*, Vol. 28, No. 2, pp. 55–60.

Dearing, R (1994) *The National Curriculum and Its Assessment.* London: HMSO.

Department for Education (1994) *Code of Practice on the Identification and Assessment of Special Educational Needs.* London: HMSO.

Department of Education and Science (1970) *Education (Handicapped Children) Act.* London: HMSO.

Department of Education and Science (1978) *Special Educational Needs: Report of the Committee of Enquiry into the Handicapped Children and Young People* (The Warnock Report). London: HMSO.

Department of Education and Science (1982) *Education Act.* London: HMSO.

Department of Education and Science (1985) *White Paper.* London: HMSO.

Department of Education and Science (1988) *Education Act.* London: HMSO.

Department for Education and Employment (1996) *National Curriculum.* London: DfEE.

Department for Education and Employment (1997) *Excellence for All Children: Meeting Special Educational Needs.* London: DfEE.

Department for Education and Employment (1998a) *Meeting Special Educational Needs: A Programme of Action.* London: DfEE.

Department for Education and Employment (1998b) *Meeting the Childcare Challenge.* London: DfEE.

Department for Education and Skills (2001a) *Special Educational Needs Code of Practice.* London: HMSO .

Department for Education and Skills (2001b) *Sessional Day Care: Guidance to the National Childcare Standards.* London: DfES.

Department for Education and Skills (2003) *Every Child Matters.* London: HMSO.

Department of Health and Social Security (2001) *Disability Discrimination Act.* London: HMSO.

Dickens, M. and Denziloe, J. (1998) *All Together: How to Create Inclusive Services for Disabled Children and their Families.* London: National Early Years Network.

Fitton, P. (1994) *Listen to Me: Communicating the Needs of People with Profound Intellectual and Multiple Disabilities.* London: Jessica Kingsley.

Gardner, H. (1991) *The Unschooled Mind: How Children Learn and How Schools Should Teach.* New York: Basic Books.

Hughes, G. (1998) 'A Suitable Case for Treatment? Constructions of Disability', in Saraga, E. (ed.) *Embodying the Social Constructions of Difference.* London: Routledge.

Jones, F. (2003) *Tools for Teaching Discipline: Instruction–Motivation.* Santa Cruz, CA: Fredric H. Jones and Associates Inc.

Jones, P. and Swain, J. (1999) 'Teachers Reviewing Annual Reviews', *British Journal of Special Education,* Vol. 26, No. 2.

Lacey, P. (1991) 'Managing the Classroom Environment', in Tilstone, T. (ed.) *Teaching Pupils with Severe Learning Difficulties: Practical Approaches.* London: David Fulton.

McQuail, S. and Pugh, G. (1995) *Effective Organisation of Early Childhood Services.* London: NCB.

Mittler, P. (2000) *Working Towards Inclusive Education: Social Contexts.* London: David Fulton.

Moss, P. and Pence, A. (1994) *Valuing Quality Early Childhood Services: New Approaches to Defining Quality.* London: Paul Chapman.

Murray, P. and Penman, J. (1996) *Let Our Children Be.* Sheffield: Parents with Attitude.

O'Brien, T. (2002) *Inclusive Childcare for Infants and Toddlers.* London: Paul Chapman

Odom, S., Wolery, R., Lieber, J., Sandall, S., Hanson, M., Beckman, P., Schwartz, I. and Horn, E. (2000) *Preschool Inclusion: A Review of Research from an Ecological Systems Perspective.* USA: Early Childhood Research Institute on Inclusion.

Oliver, M. (1996) 'Understanding Disability: From Theory to Practice', in Swain, J., Finkelstein, V., French, S. and Oliver, M. (eds), *Disabling Barriers: Enabling Environments.* London: Sage/Open University Press.

Osgood, J. and Sharp, C. (2000) *Developing Early Education and Childcare Services for the 21st Century.* Berkshire: NFER.

Ouvrey, C. and Saunders, S. (1996) 'Pupils with Profound and Multiple Learning Difficulties', in Carpenter, B., Ashdown, R. and Bovair, K. (1996) *Enabling Access.* London: David Fulton.

Pascal, C. and Bertram, T. (2001) *Effective Early Learning: Case Studies in Improvement.* London: Paul Chapman.

PIVATS (2000) *Performance Indicators for Value Added Target Setting.* Preston: Lancashire County Council.

QCA (2001) *Planning, Teaching and Assessing the Curriculum for Pupils with Learning Difficulties.* London: DfEE.

Reiser, R. and Mason, M. (1992) *Disability Equality in the Classroom: A Human Rights Issue.* London: Disability Equality in Education.

Rose, R., Fletcher, W. and Goodwin, G. (1999) 'Pupils with Severe Learning Difficulties as Personal Target Setters', *British Journal of Special Education*, Vol. 26, No. 4, pp. 206–12.

Somogyvary, B. (1986) in Wade, B. and Moore, M. (1993) *Experiencing Special Education: What Young People with Special Educational Needs Can Tell Us.* Buckingham: Open University Press.

Souza, A. (1996) 'Inclusive Education Conference Statement', in Murray, P. and Penman, J. *Let Our Children Be: A Collection of Stories.* Sheffield: Parents with Attitude.

Swain, J., Gillman, M. and French, S. (1998) *Confronting Disabling Barriers: Towards Making Organisations Accessible.* Birmingham: Venture Press.

Thomas, G. and Loxley, A. (2001) *Deconstructing Special Education and Constructing Inclusion.* Buckingham: Open University Press.

Vygotsky, L. S. (1978) *Mind in Society.* Cambridge, MA: Harvard University Press.

Wade, B. and Moore, M. (1993) *Experiencing Special Education: What Young People with Special Educational Needs Can Tell Us.* Buckingham: Open University Press.

Wolfendale, S. (2000) 'Special Needs in Early Years: Prospects for Policy and Practice', *Support for Learning*, Vol. 15, No. 4, November.

Index